Rival States, Rival Firms: How Do People Fit In?

The Global Unemployment Challenge

Isabelle Grunberg

United Nations Development Programme
Office of Development Studies
Discussion Paper Series

Contents

Foreword

The end of the 20th century finds us having great difficulty reconciling economic goals and human objectives. In many countries we find that positive economic forces (income expansion, a strong currency, a trade surplus, financially healthy enterprises) coexist with stagnating—and at times deteriorating—human and social indicators: poverty persists, income inequality is getting worse in many parts of the world and unemployment continues to be high, even rising in many industrial countries. This suggests that present economic strategies may be promoting "jobless growth", leading to the reversal of previous gains in human development.

But the end of the 20th century is also having unprecedented economic liberalization and internationalization of markets combined with increasing globalization of developmental problems, ranging from cross-border effects of poverty and environmental degradation to international spill overs on national monetary and fiscal policies (notably interest rate policies). The new openness of countries has sharpened the competition among enterprises and states. The demands that global capital markets impose on states—in ensuring macroeconomic stability and financial credibility—have never been greater. This poses the vexing question: where do people fit in?

This paper by Isabelle Grunberg addresses this question, tackling unemployment. It shows how incentives for states and firms in the global economy drive a wedge between economic processes and human goals. She argues that efficiency and human development (in this case, improved opportunities for meaningful work) are reconcilable goals. But they cannot be achieved without a thorough—and probably agonizing—reappraisal of today's policy assumptions and strategies. National policy instruments must be adjusted to the new global policy context and complemented by coordinated global action. Grunberg proposes a policy agenda for further discussion and research.

The preliminary findings presented here are intended as the starting point for a systematic dialogue with specialists and policy-makers in developing and industrial countries. We welcome any observations and comments you may have. And we would be grateful if you would share with us relevant studies that you may have undertaken on this topic—studies we would be happy to consider for publication in our Discussion Paper series.

A second version of this paper, enriched by extensive consultation, will be published towards the end of 1996. It is hoped that this and further studies on this theme will foster the elaboration of effective policy options in this crucial area of global unemployment—and help clarify the wider issue of how to achieve greater consistency between economic growth, human goals and environmental sustainability.

Inge Kaul
Director
Office of Development Studies
New York, January 1996

I.
Human Development and Policy-Making in the Global Economy

T his study is an exploration of the constraints and incentives facing people-centered development policies.[1] Its aim is to analyse what are perceived by many as increasing signs that the present international political economy is dysfunctional in terms of pursuing sustainable human development. In order to do so, the study focuses on the issue of unemployment, which is construed as having two sides: a quantitative side—the lack of jobs—and a qualitative side—the disappearance of "good jobs", that is, of employment that is stable, productive and remunerative.

More broadly, this dysfunction hampers people's participation in development. We are currently witnessing a situation in which policy-makers are increasingly constrained in putting into place a people-oriented policy framework—and citizens feel increasingly out of control.

Indeed, even though citizens in individual countries may wish to implement, or preserve, policies that enhance human well-being or that protect the most vulnerable members of society, they are being told that overriding international constraints make the exercise of such a choice impossible. In particular they are told that higher unemployment will result if social safety nets are not phased out. The slogan "There is no alternative" (to dis-

1

mantling the welfare state), which gained prominence in the 1980s, seems to encapsulate this predicament and to ultimately undermine the essence of democracy itself. Indeed, the idea that "the *consumer* has a choice" has justified widespread privatization, deregulation, and enhanced competition in world markets; but in the process the notion that "the *citizen* has a choice" has been lost. This loss may explain the current decline of political participation in advanced democracies, the growing cynicism about the power of governments to improve people's lives, and the rise of nationalist and fundamentalist ideologies. Even though formal democracy has made considerable headway in recent years, its content—the ability of citizens to shape the values that guide policy choices—has been increasingly weakened.

The fact that the world economy is now showing signs of being dysfunctional reminds us that markets are human institutions and need to operate within a political and legal framework. In the relatively closed economies of the past, a balance between states and markets was achieved at the national level. National authorities could reap the efficiency benefits of markets, while controlling and compensating for their potential divisiveness. But now there is a growing discrepancy between an economy that is more and more international, and a policy-making structure and civil society that are still largely fragmented among states. The effects of this distortion can be observed in many different areas. Therefore, in view of the challenge posed by growing unemployment and inequality, a new paradigm that focuses our thinking on the global arena is urgently needed so that citizens in both industrial and developing countries can regain control over their future.

The meaning of "work": a methodological note
The notions of "job", "employment" and "work" are currently undergoing drastic revision. Calls are being made to enlarge the definition of work in mainstream economic analysis and national accounting to include unremunerated activities such as volunteer work, domestic work, and community activities, such as those performed by retired persons. In developing countries the "Northern" model of formal, contractual work relations between employees and employers represents only a very small portion of all work activities—and a bad proxy for activities such as subsistence agriculture. In these situations, the promising concept of "sustainable livelihoods" as a general policy goal has been put forward.

The present study, however, largely relies on that work that is remunerated. Our (admittedly narrow) starting point is where human lives intersect with the logic of the market.

This choice does not in any way reflect a value preference for remunerated rather than unremunerated labour. It also does not imply that unremunerated work is irrelevant for the study of remunerated work. This choice is made simply because of methodological expediency. As the study attempts to show, the tools of conventional economics are in constant need of updating. New concepts and methods are constantly being devised to understand an extremely complex reality. In particular, one needs to go beyond strictly market economics, to integrate the behaviour and mutual interaction of both market and nonmarket actors, of states as well as firms. Hence the methodology used here is that of international political economy, in particular as developed by Susan Strange.[2] Within this framework the study attempts to delineate mutual cause-and-effect relationships, to analyse key global mechanisms and their effects on employment and human development, and, in particular, to present for debate a new concept of "structural demand shortfall", which goes beyond a pure business-cycle view of aggregate demand.

Including unremunerated work in the analysis, however, would mean a radical departure from the methodology of international political economy. To start with, the notion of "work" would need to be defined, and this definition would need to be comprehensive without being vague. A vital component of such a framework would have to be cultural anthropology, analysing the flow of nonmonetary rewards (whether symbolic or material) in a society. This opens up fascinating avenues. Yet issues such as child labour could not be analysed in such a framework. Studying is work, as going to school. In that sense, even children who do not work in the traditional sense, work. Hence in the absence of a readily available framework the choice that has been made here is to pursue theoretical innovation, but not at the expense of policy relevance.

2.
The Twin Challenges
of Global Unemployment

A t first sight, global unemployment refers to the fact that a substantial portion of the world labour force is out of work. Yet, in some situations a purely quantitative approach does not adequately reflect a situation in which many workers have traded stable, productive, and remunerative employment for work that makes them feel increasingly vulnerable. Students of unemployment issues are therefore challenged to address this qualitative dimension of the problem. In recent years this challenge has given rise to studies exploring "disguised unemployment", or to studies focusing on the problem of the "working poor".[3]

This section offers a brief account of the two faces of unemployment, using United States and European experiences as illustrations. It also reviews the determinants of employment in developing countries.

THE RISE OF JOBLESSNESS

The phenomenon
Despite growth in world output in recent years (2.6% in 1994, 2.75% in 1995) and a sharp increase in world trade (9.5% in 1994), the problem of global unemployment remains acute. In most countries, including the richest, employment has been stagnating since the 1970s and an ever-higher proportion of the workforce has been idle.[4]

Between 1960–73 and 1988–94 the unemployment rate has grown 1.8 times in Canada, 2 times in Italy and Japan, 4 times in the United Kingdom, 5 times in France, and 8.5 times in Germany[5]. Western Europe is a critical illustration of the phenomenon of "jobless growth" analysed in the 1993 Human Development Report. [6] Six million jobs were lost in the European Union (EU) between 1991 and 1994[7]. Yet, during this period growth was positive, albeit low (average GDP growth was 1%).[8] The trend has been less severe in the United States, with growth in the unemployment rate of 1.2% during the same period.

For the developing world such long-term trends are more difficult to document because of statistical gaps. But the recent trends are just as worrying. In Sub-Saharan Africa paid employment in manufacturing declined at a rate of 0.5% per year during the 1980s, and urban unemployment now ranges between 15% and 20% of the workforce, compared with around 10% in the mid-1970s.[9] In Latin America paid employment fell at a rate of about 0.1% per year during the 1980s.[10]

In transition economies the picture is even more dramatic. Within three years, 1990 to 1993, unemployment rose by 150% in Poland, by 340% in the Czech Republic and by 560% in Hungary.[11]

The growth of unemployment following the global oil crises of the 1970s could be laid at the door of these exogenous shocks. But with the persistence of the problem more than twenty years hence, many analysts are suspecting that the unemployment crisis, far from being cyclical or accidental, is becoming a permanent feature of the world economy, raising alarming questions about longer-term prospects.

Some countries, however, distinguished themselves by the improvement they were able to achieve in their employment situations. China and East and South-East Asian countries saw employment grow by 2.3% to 5.9% a year in the 1980s.[12] In South Asia manufacturing jobs grew by an average of 1% a year between 1981 and 1990.[13] The United States has managed to maintain its rate of unemployment fluctuating around 6% in the last two decades. This low rate, however, has been achieved at a cost—real incomes of the poorest people have fallen, and inequality has markedly worsened since the 1960s.

The puzzle of joblessness
Explanations have been advanced and models have been tested to explain jobless growth and divisive growth. (They will be discussed in later sections.)

The unemployment problem, however, remains a mystery. High rates of unemployment mean that more people would like to contribute to the production of more goods and services. Yet, the same people are also looking to earn more, to acquire more purchasing power, in short, to also be consumers of goods and services. The paradox is that those who are looking for jobs are looking to be both producers and consumers. If so, why can they not produce the very goods and services that they (or millions of others like them) would like to consume? Why can they not, as a group, increase their income by working, thereby increasing the demand for goods and services by becoming consumers themselves? In other words, why is it that two needs that are evidently complementary—the need to have a productive occupation and the need to purchase more goods and services—do not fulfil each other?

There is indeed something "economically irrational" about the current unemployment situation, to quote a recent report by the International Labour Organization.[14] Various economists will provide different answers to this paradox, stressing the supply or the demand side of the equation. The fact that global unemployment has worsened relentlessly, however, shows that labour market studies, and indeed economic science as a whole, have yet failed to answer these basic questions.

THE TRADE-OFF BETWEEN EMPLOYMENT AND EQUITY

Labour market economists do tend to agree with a set of prescriptions that would enhance the flexibility of the market place and remove obstacles to hiring and firing and to the downward movements of wages. These analysts recommend more flexible work hours and phasing out unemployment insurance and other income alternatives to work.[15] When they have been applied, however, these measures have increased inequality and have failed to stem the loss of "good jobs"—stable, remunerative, full-time employment. The results have been both a wider gap between the best-paid and the lowest-paid jobs (that is, an increase in wage dispersion), and a larger share of the workforce holding low-wage jobs.[16]

In the United Kingdom, the gap between the highest and the lowest paid male workers is at its widest since the 1880s, when such figures were first compiled.[17]

The phenomenon

The rise of the working poor is well documented. In the United States many families with at least one full-time income fall below the poverty line. In fact, the number of such families has risen from 1.6 million in 1980 to 2.1 million in 1990.[18] Most newly created jobs do not carry employment security, health insurance, or other benefits such as paid leave or pension plans. These new jobs are poorly paid and are often part-time. In France, for example, the proportion of jobs that are part-time has grown from 3% in 1983 to 8.5% in 1991.

In turn, growing wage inequalities are fueling a wider gap between rich and poor in all industrial economies. In the United States the poorest have grown poorer in absolute terms in the past two decades, with the families in the poorest decile experiencing a drop in real income of 11% between 1973 and 1992.[19] This phenomenon of "divisive growth" or "impoverishing growth" contrasts with the period 1950–70, when the benefits of growth were more equally distributed.

The same phenomenon is observable in most developing countries, where a growing gap between the highest paid and the lowest paid is often accompanied by a decline in real wages paid to unskilled workers. In Latin America the Gini coefficient measuring income inequality rose from 0.51 to 0.57 in the 1980s, while poverty levels increased and consumption per capita fell.[20] According to World Bank projections to 2000, which extrapolate from present trends, Latin American workers will see a real wage gain of 45% or a wage loss of 3%, depending on whether they are skilled or not. In the Middle East and North Africa the gains for skilled workers will be 27%, but unskilled workers will suffer a 2% cut in real wages. Although real wage cuts are expected to be limited to these two regions, a gap between trends in wages for skilled and unskilled workers will remain in all developing economies.[21] "There is substantial risk," writes the World Bank, "that inequality between rich and poor [in all countries] will grow over the coming decade, while poverty deepens".[22]

The experiences of industrial countries and the correlation found between job creation and wage dispersion suggest that job creation exacts a price in terms of income inequality, and therefore, potentially, social cohesion. This relationship creates a policy dilemma for decision-makers, in that the unemployment problem has two faces: a quantitative one—the stagnation in the number of jobs—and a qualitative one—falling wages and growing inequality that accompany job creation.[23] Some studies have even suggested that low-wage employment may actually reduce total output by reducing the productivity of workers.[24]

The "European disease" versus the "United States disease"

The United States and the countries of the European Union may be used as examples. Although they represent a limited sample of the world, they offer "ideal" situations that are useful in understanding the dilemmas facing other economies. Their policy choices are also important in evaluating the type of development path, or model, against which developing countries will assess their own objectives and strategies. The problem of unemployment in developing countries per se will be analysed subsequently.

The contrast between what has become known as Europe's unemployment problem and the sustained job creation observable in the United States—though at the price of a deterioration in the quality of jobs—is probably a result of European social policies that both guarantee decent terms of employment for those who hold jobs and a social safety net for those who do not. The downside is that these policies increase the cost to firms of hiring additional labour and decrease incentives for workers to accept jobs that are available.

As a result, European firms have tended to invest in production methods with a higher technological content—the ratio of capital to labour used in production has sharply increased compared with the United States. Hence labour productivity has grown much faster in Europe than in the United States. Between 1988 and 1992, for example, the average annual growth of productivity has been close to 2% in France, Germany, Italy, and Japan, compared with 0.6% in the United States and 0.4% in the United Kingdom.[25] And this development is not new—since 1961 United States productivity growth has consistently been half of the lowest figure found in Europe (except in the United Kingdom). In turn, lower productivity growth often means lower wages, hence the stagnation of real wages in the United States compared with Western European countries (figure 2.1).[26]

This pattern is consistent with the picture of jobs (in the low-income brackets) that are better paid, though rarer, in the European Community and with the correlation that researchers have found between higher labour productivity and higher wage equality.[27]

The contrast in the employment situation between Europe and the United States illustrates the new dilemma faced by policy-makers that is becoming a structural feature of the world economy. The European and United States situations illustrate two different ways of adjusting to the same underlying constraints, and, in a broader sense, two kinds of devel-

Figure 2.1 Real wages and labour productivity, industrialized countries, 1974–94

(Average annual growth rate, in percent)

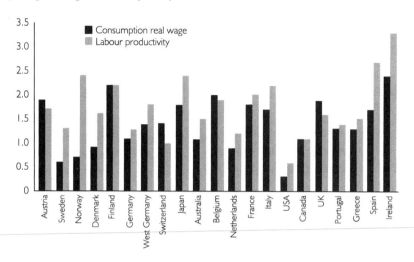

Source: Organisation of Economic Co-operation and Development, Economic Outlook (June 1994), and reference supplement.

opment strategies that cut across North-South divides. Former United States Labour Secretary Ray Marshall, for example, writes that in the global competitive environment countries in both the South and the North respond either with lower wages or by focusing on productivity and quality. He notes that "most high-income developed countries, and some of the top-performing developing countries in Asia have either implicitly or explicitly rejected the low-wage option."[28] Thus the relevance of these categories to the experiences of developing countries is greater than a casual observation would lead one to believe.

Yet, in the long run even the low-wage option is no guarantee of low unemployment. There is limited evidence emerging, showing that the United States is also undergoing a "jobless recovery". *Fortune* reports that in 1994 the profits of the top 500 companies in the world grew by 62.1%, while employment only grew by 3.1%.[29] International comparisons show that such a shortfall in employment creation in this recovery compared with the last one (what one may call "short-term jobless growth") was at least as pronounced in the United States as in other OECD countries.[30] In a systematic comparison of profit and employment indicators in the present recovery (which began in 1991) and previous ones, *Business Week* found a systematic trend towards higher corporate profits, lower rates of increase in household incomes, and lower rates of employment recovery.[31]

Thus it appears that, even though the United States paid the price in terms of higher inequality and real decreases of lower wages, it may be also experiencing jobless growth. United States workers could be presented with the worse of both worlds—"European" rise in unemployment and "US" rise in poverty and inequality. This outcome casts doubt on the widely held view that the solution to unemployment lies in the deregulation of labour markets and the phasing out of social safety nets.[32]

Therefore, labour market economics alone does not provide a real-world answer to the complex problem of global unemployment, because the effectiveness of its policy recommendations are in doubt and because many of these recommendations are not conducive to the promotion of sustainable human development. Indeed, the scaling back of social policies that some argue are the price for better employment performance directly challenges the principles laid out, for example, in the International Declaration of Human Rights (which, in article 25, provides for the attainment of such goals as a just remuneration for labour, education, or "the right to security in the event of unemployment, sickness, disability, widowhood, old age"). If such goals are allowed to wither away, the meaning of development itself could be lost.

SPECIAL FEATURES OF DEVELOPING COUNTRIES

A criticism made of many of the generalizations on work or employment is that they use industrial countries and their labour markets as paradigms. The present study is not immune from this criticism. Developing countries are seen as variants of, or deviations from, the Western model. Yet in some ways the reverse may be true. The highly dualistic employment situation in developing countries may be becoming a model, around which other economies converge. Likewise, the notion of "disguised unemployment", originally conceived as applying to developing countries (see below), is becoming a useful tool for understanding employment issues in developed countries. It is hoped that this and further studies will stimulate debate among economists in both developing and industrial countries as to whether or not generalizations can be made that cut across their divide. For the time being, however, we will outline specific areas in which the employment problem in developing countries differs from that in industrial countries.

Sustained employment creation in newly industrializing countries
Developing countries present a very unequal picture when it comes to employment trends. Standing in contrast to the decline of employment observed in Africa and the stagnation in Latin America and South Asia, is the sustained employment boom observed in East and South-East Asia. In East and South-East Asia total employment grew rapidly in the 1980s (from a 2.3% annual growth rate in Hong Kong to 5.9% in Singapore), mainly in the manufacturing sector; this growth was accompanied by a rise in incomes and a decline in poverty. Hence these countries avoided the trade-off often observed between employment creation and equity.

These positive outcomes were achieved with a combination of high savings rates, export-oriented strategy, tight management of inward investment, and successful industrial policies. Intertemporal and international comparisons in the region show that trade unions and labour laws did not adversely affect growth, but contributed to a more equitable distribution of the wealth created by growth.[33]

The newly industrializing countries (NICs) of East and South-East Asia were able to move up the product cycle by developing an indigenous technological capability and by investing in education. This move was necessary in order to resist competition from a second tier of NICs that offered comparable or lower wages.

The success of the NICs has prompted policy-makers to recommend a mix of export-orientation and good domestic economic management.[34] There has been a debate, however, as to how sustainable and replicable the South-East Asian model is. Recent studies have tended to emphasize the role of public authorities in steering this process.[35]

The sharply unequal performance of developing economies when it comes to employment is a reminder that international trade and competition have polarizing effects among states as well as among firms. The effects are evident among firms in the ongoing process of industrial restructuring whereby uncompetitive firms disappear or merge. Among states they are seen in the logic of specialization and concentration of production, whereby manufacturing, for example, will coalesce in a small number of export processing zones, or in countries that offer a good investment climate and a high-productivity, low-wage work force. The concentration of production in the most competitive economies will occur until labour shortages appear, causing wages to rise and low-skilled production to relocate elsewhere, creating new policy challenges for maturing economies.

Disguised unemployment in other economies
Employment statistics in developing countries are notoriously difficult to collect and compare because they often refer to the type of full-time employment found in industrial countries. In developing countries this type of employment is found mostly in the modern sector, and it coexists with a large portion of rural, self-employed artisans or farmers, or providers of petty services in the cities. Disguised unemployment, or underemployment, refers to this type of low-income, low-productivity work. By contrast, the formal sector tends to offer higher wages and benefits.[36]

The informal sector is predominantly urban in Latin America and rural in Africa and South Asia. In Latin America, for example, 32% of nonagricultural employment is tied to the informal sector.[37]

This duality reflects the nature of most economies in the developing world, with an outward-looking sector (often composed of multinational companies) superimposed on traditional ways of life. The modern sector tends to have a pull effect on underemployed labour, which is often reflected in urban migration. The supply of jobs is, however, often insufficient, and a large number of migrants find themselves relegated to the margins of the modern economy. Hence there are two kinds of underemployed: those who remain in their traditional occupations and those who are eking out a living at the periphery of the modern sector (as street vendors, car window cleaners, shoe polishers, improvised tourist guides and so on). For the latter, Marx's metaphor of a "reserve army" of workers is suggestive, especially because labour, having been mobilized from traditional, rural employment, may find itself abruptly "demobilized" by downturns in business cycles or cuts in public-sector employment.

Thus although the modern sector offers the promise of higher wages and productivity, it also makes workers more vulnerable to external shocks, such as abrupt changes in the prices of internationally traded goods, or currency crises, exemplified by that of the Mexican peso. Moreover, demographics in developing countries are such that the maintenance of low-productivity jobs acts as a safety net. Many economists advocate the enhancement of rural employment (through help for the small-farm sector) for this reason, as well as a way to prevent the drift to the cities and its attendant social dislocation.[38]

The importance of culture
Quantitative data and labour statistics must be complemented by an awareness that work everywhere is embedded in a set of social relationships, traditions, representations, and values. The following anecdote is an illustration.

In Bombay, India, thousands of men called *dabbawallahs* travel each day between suburban homes and the city, carrying home-made lunches to office workers, then returning the empty containers to their wives. The lunches, packed in tall, round tins are carefully marked, numbered and distributed, and carried on large wooden trays through suburban trains and office buildings. The tradition dates back to the days of the Raj, and has become a customary practice in Bombay, helping to keep local food habits alive and to provide work for hundreds of otherwise unemployed men. Lunches could probably be provided more cheaply, but the system is perfectly efficient when local customs and the availability of labour are taken into account. This practice reflects a social consensus whereby the needs of office workers meet the needs of unemployed people in ways that cannot be captured in standard economic theory—which would simply stress the income foregone by office workers who failed to chose the most cost-efficient solution.[39]

Development strategies that overlook these complex webs of tradition and interdependencies in favour of a unidimensional quest for higher growth and income run the risk, not only of putting material pursuits before human needs and collective identities, but of creating a backlash—currently observed in the widespread resurgence of nationalism or religious fundamentalism—and therefore of becoming unsustainable in the long term.

Also, societies value formal employment to a varying degree. Although cultural factors can slow down the pace of industrialization (anecdotal evidence, for example, points to a difficult match between the traditional upbringing of boys in Maghreb countries and the work methods and discipline demanded by modern manufacturing) in some countries, in others tradition places high value on formal employment. For example, in an ominous quote borrowed from a famous Moldovan poet, the 1995 National

Human Development Report for the Republic of Moldova warns that unemployment "can lead to social degeneration, which can lead to political instability, and ultimately revolution."[40] Labour policies must be framed in this context, too.

3.
The Causes of Global Unemployment

Although figures show a global increase in joblessness, the phenomenon could result from the aggregation of very different situations across regions and countries. Also what passes as an inexorable drift may be the coincidence of short- to medium-term trends—trends that are potentially reversible.

SHORT-TERM AND MEDIUM-TERM CAUSES
In the absence of foresight the distinction between medium- and long-term causes is not an easy one to make. Nevertheless, we can identify trends that have been at work in the last ten to fifteen years or that may recede in the next ten to fifteen years.

Currency constraints in industrialized countries
In Western Europe the move towards a unified market and common institutions has boosted investment and has been credited with an improvement in the employment situation in the second half of the 1980s. The European project, however, is fraught with obstacles to job creation, at least in the short term.

First, pan-European consolidation and concentration between firms to service the larger market has meant more job shedding. More significantly, plans for a European Monetary Union (EMU) have taken a considerable toll on employment. The formation of a European Monetary Union will culminate in a single European currency—a very favourable outcome for employment, because it will improve resource allocation and facilitate trade. But a common currency is being created through economic "convergence", whereby inflation rates and public deficits are kept under tight control (the Maastricht Treaty holds that countries will need to trim their budget deficits to 3% of GDP and reduce public-sector debt to below 60% of GDP in order to be eligible for participation in the monetary union). The ensuing squeeze on public spending and consumption has imparted a deflationary bias to European economies, resulting in employment stagnation. It is estimated that full implementation of the Maastricht criteria will result in a loss of one million jobs by the turn of the century. Conversely, 200,000 jobs would be created if monetary union were achieved without the Maastricht criteria.[41]

Moreover, in the past fifteen years, the European Monetary System (EMS) has required most governments to ensure that their currencies stay within 15% of agreed central rates. In practice, this means that all EMS members have had to adjust to the persistent strength of the German mark by maintaining high rates of interest, and thus overvalued parities.

Since 1991 the spending requirements of German unification have led the Bundesbank to maintain a high rate of interest on the German currency in order to attract investors and prevent inflation—again boosting the exchange rate. In order to prevent their currencies from falling too low in relation to the mark, other European countries have had to match interest rate increases on the mark with similar increases on their own currencies. High interest rates are notoriously inimical to employment because they delay investment decisions and divert capital away from productive investment and into financial markets.

The fact that the trend towards forming a closer European union has worsened the unemployment problem in Europe seems ironic. But this suspicion is reinforced by the fact that those countries that are either outside of the EU, such as Norway and Switzerland or that joined the EU recently, such as Austria or Sweden, have fared much better than their neighbours in terms of employment, with an average unemployment rate less than 2% before 1981, and less than 8% thereafter (6% excluding Sweden), compared with 10–11% in the European Union.[42]

The problem of monetary constraints on growth should in theory subside after the completion of monetary union. Still, it is likely that fiscal and monetary policies will continue to be fairly restrictive since the management of the new currency will closely follow practices that have until now governed the German mark. The new system may be even more deflationary than the present one, as penalties are being envisaged for states that fail to keep budget deficits below an agreed maximum. This policy would be tantamount to carrying the painful transitional period into an indeterminate future. European workers would pay the full price, yet get none of the potential benefits, of the single currency.

In Japan joblessness reached postwar records of 3.4% in 1995. Once again, this rate is largely due to monetary factors—the yen rose by 20% against the dollar between January and April 1995, with the dollar dipping below 80 yen. A strong yen hurts exports, hence output growth, hence employment.[43]

Although the Japanese unemployment rate is very small in comparison with Europe's 11%, the unprecedented figure has alarmed manufacturers and policy-makers.[44]

Industrial dislocation in transition economies

The dramatic rise in unemployment in Eastern European countries and the countries of the former Soviet Union is largely due to the 20–30% fall in output observed between 1990 and 1993.[45] This fall is explained by large-scale industrial restructuring and the shedding of uncompetitive activities. In Eastern Europe the collapse of trade within the former Council for Mutual Economic Assistance (CMEA) has meant a loss of income and external markets. The dislocation of the whole system of centrally planned production has come at a time when the private sector was not ready to step in because of unclear property rights and lack of familiarity with management methods in a free market environment.

The unemployment problem in transition economies is causing hardship and uncertainty, and is undermining the social and political consensus that paved the way for a democratic, free market society, as recent elections have shown. Optimists argue, though, that the problem is transitional, and that economic progress will follow in the wake of this adjustment crisis.[46]

Structural adjustment in developing countries

The programmes of structural adjustment undertaken by most developing countries in the 1980s could create sharp rises in unemployment, at least in the short term. The cut in public spending and downsizing or privatization of publicly owned firms, restrictive monetary policies, and price increases of imports as a result of devaluation all demobilize labour and curb demand and investment.

In Argentina for example, unemployment reached a record 18.6% in 1995, rising from 10.5% in 1994. This increase followed an economic plan that included a sharply restrictive monetary stance.[47] By contrast, Argentina's rate of unemployment was 2.5% on average throughout the 1970s. In the long run such trends should be reversed by an increase in exports, although this outcome has been very unequal across countries.[48]

Thus there are good explanations as to why global employment is stagnant in the 1990s. But looking beyond what may seem a coincidence of unhappy circumstances, more and more analysts are searching for long-term trends that will affect our projections of the future. There are, in fact, common threads among these situations, and what passed as temporary adjustment policies have become a structural feature of the contemporary world economy, affecting both industrial and developing economies.

LONG-TERM TRENDS AND STRUCTURAL CAUSES

This section reviews the global factors that may be responsible for the problem of unemployment. It hypothesizes that the unemployment problem is due to a global or regional mismatch between the supply of and demand for workers, and reviews the possibility that an excessive supply of workers may be at the root of the problem. It then moves to explanations that focus on an insufficient demand for labour.

An increased supply of workers

The role of demographic trends. The rate of employment is largely affected by the number of new entrants into the labour market. Even if a large number of new jobs are created in an economy, they may be outnumbered by the tide of new people seeking work. This pattern is seen in the short run (and is a reason why governments calculate seasonally adjusted rates of unemployment). More broadly, unequal employment performance in developing countries can to some extent be explained by different rates of population growth. For example, the employment prospects of South Asia are lower than those of South-East Asia because the South Asian labour force is projected to grow by 2.1% per year for the rest of the decade and beyond. At this growth rate more than 10 million new workers will be looking for jobs every year. In comparison, the total number of jobs available in the modern sector was about 60 million at the end of the 1980s. Similarly, the outlook for employment growth in Africa is marred by the fact that the continent has the highest rate of population and labour force growth.[49]

In the long run, however, it is unclear how important a role demographics plays in the job equation. In theory, a larger population means an increased demand for goods and services, and therefore expanded markets and expanded opportunities for businesses and workers. A gap may be created if goods and services are produced with less labour or if other factors interfere with the feed-back loop between consumption and production. But after necessary adjustments are made, the size of the population itself should not be a predominant factor.

Women's increased participation in the labour force. The fact that more women—who are already consumers—are looking for formal sector jobs could contribute to the long-term rise in unemployment. Indeed, between 1970 and 1990 women's average share in the labour force increased by 9%, to 42% in Western Europe, the United States and other industrial countries. In Northern Africa, Latin America, the Caribbean and Southern Asia the increase has been higher than 10%. In Sub-Saharan Africa, by contrast, there has been a marked decrease in the participation rate of women, from 57% to 53% (figure 3.1).

The scope of the labour supply change should not be exaggerated, though. After all, the highest average regional rate of growth in women's participation is around 10% over a twenty-year period. In comparison, increases in the unemployment rate within a comparable time span (between 1960–1973 and 1988–1994) ranged from 80% in the United States to 850% in Germany.[50]

Moreover, there does not seem to be a clear correlation in timing between this phenomenon and the worldwide rise in unemployment. Indeed, women's participation rates increased much more in the 1980s than in the 1970s in all regions—in the industrial world, for example, by 5–6 percentage points in the 1970s, and 8–9 percentage points in the 1980s.[51] By contrast, the sharpest rise in unemployment occurred after the first oil shock (figure 3.2).

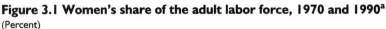

Figure 3.1 Women's share of the adult labor force, 1970 and 1990[a]
(Percent)

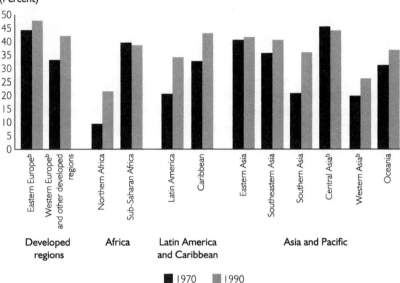

■ 1970　▧ 1990

a. Estimates for 1990 based on national population census and survey data as reported by countries and not adjusted for comparability to internationally recommended definitions.
b. Figures for 1970 include ILO estimates for states succeeding the former Soviet Union.
Source: For 1970, prepared by the Statistical Division of the United Nations Secretariat from estimated economically active population in *Economically Active Population—Estimates, 1950–1980, Projections, 1985–2025.* Six volumes. Geneva: International Labour Organization. 1986). For 1990, prepared by the Statistical Division from ILO, *Year Book of Labour Statistics,* various years up to 1993 (Geneva) and national census and survey reports.

Moreover, there is evidence that women's participation in the labour market occurs more in response to economic incentives and employment opportunities than to exogenous changes in norms and values. Economic growth increases the rate of women's participation, while economic contractions lower it. For example, in many developing regions and in Eastern Europe, economic adjustment programmes and contractions in public spending have led to overall declines in employment opportunities—with a resulting net decline in women's participation rate.[52]

Thus the social and cultural changes that have led more women to seek formal employment in many countries has not been a major factor in the global rise of unemployment. The answer, therefore, must lie in a reduced overall demand for labour.

Figure 3.2 EU unemployment rate

(per cent)

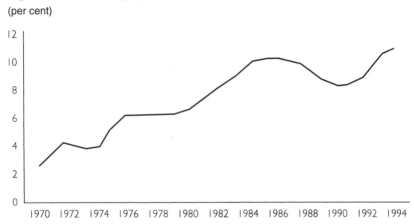

Source: OECD. Reproduced from "Survey of the European Union". *The Economist,* 22 October 1994. p. 4.

A decreased demand for workers

Three structural changes in the global political economy, including, in particular, increased rivalry between states and between firms, seem to be at the root of the apparent stagnation in demand for workers. Before analysing these three changes, however, this section begins by reviewing two habitual suspects: international trade is often blamed for a loss of low-skilled jobs in high-income countries, and technology is held responsible for net job losses and for increasing inequality. Traditionally, however, there has been a quasi-consensus among professional economists that neither international trade nor technology hurts employment. A more nuanced view is now emerging, especially with regard to the effects of technological advances in the way goods and services are produced.

We show that, more than trade or technology, what matters is the political and macroeconomic environment in which these developments occur: in the absence of corrective policies, technological advances could increase wage dispersion. In the context of sluggish consumer demand, both trade and technology will simply redistribute wealth and jobs, and the potential they hold for increased efficiency and wealth creation could be lost.

International trade. Recent debates on the unemployment problem in Western economies have focused on the threat to workers from imports of cheap manufactured goods produced by low-cost producers in industrializing economies. This competition reduces the demand for low-skilled labour in the North, resulting in either unemployment or wage stagnation and decline. Indeed, economic theory predicts that under free trade conditions, the remuneration of inputs (capital, workers, land) will equalize across countries. This means that in the long run, assuming equal productivity, there will be a convergence between the wages paid in, say, the United Kingdom, and those paid in Brazil. Projections have shown that, in theory, this equalized wage level would be slightly higher than the present wages paid in Nigeria—and roughly one-fifth of the current United States wage level (figure 3.3).

Even if such predictions seem extreme, all observers, including the authors of the *World Bank Development Report 1995*, concede that free trade will bring losses for unskilled workers in the North, even though the economy as a whole will benefit. The relocation of manufacturing activities overseas is also cited as a structural factor explaining the rise of Japanese unemployment.[53]

Economists are divided, however, on the precise effects of competition from the South, and on its extent. The British economist Patrick Minford estimates that real wages for unskilled workers in the North will fall by 2% a year.[54] Adrian Wood of Sussex University notes that manufactured goods now account for more than half of exports from developing countries, compared to 5% in 1955, and estimates that this change in the composition of South-North trade accounts for almost all the collapse in the demand for unskilled labour in the North.[55]

Figure 3.3 Wages in the global labour market

1989 hourly wage (1985 dollars)

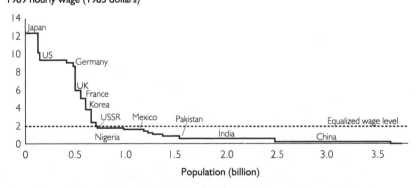

Source: Learmer, *The Hecksler–Ohlin Model in Theory and Practice*. Princeton: University Press. 1995. "Flushing out the Trade Debate". *Financial Times*, 5 June 1995.

Other economists (mainly from the United States, where workers in services now outnumber those in manufacturing) either refute the argument on the grounds that the prices of goods produced with unskilled labour have not declined in relation to the prices of goods produced with skilled labour, or reckon that international trade only explains a small portion of the wage decline—from 10% to 30%—in Northern countries.

Indeed, the manufacturing sector represents only about 20% of jobs in the OECD countries. But far from proving that the effects of international trade with newly industrializing countries are negligible, this statistic may indicate that the process of deindustrialization has already taken place.

Most economists point out that the losses experienced in one sector will be made up by gains in others. For example, even if manufacturing jobs are lost in industrialized economies through trade with and investment in newly industrializing countries, this loss will be accompanied by the development of substantial markets in the same countries for the goods (such as those with a high technological content, or capital goods) typically provided by industrial countries. Indeed, total exports to NICs have grown just as fast as imports from NICs.[56] And the Group of Seven as a whole enjoys a trade surplus with the developing world. The Swiss maker of power generation equipment Asea Brown Boveri (ABB), for example, expects Asia to account for more than half the world's demand for its machinery over the next ten years.[57]

In fact, sales to the developing world explain why US companies have fared so well in 1994 despite stagnation in the home market. In that year, for example, Citicorp made 44% of its profits from its business in the developing world. And Boeing sells one in seven of its airplanes to Chinese airlines.[58]

The problem is that such a boom in the sales of high-technology goods and services translates into higher profits, not higher rates of employment.

Technology. An unexpected outcome of this controversy has been to give a new academic respectability to the theory that technological advances, especially when applied to production processes, may be responsible for growing unemployment. This view, which has long been dismissed as the superficial observation of sensational journalists, prophets of doom, and neo-Luddites, is now being cited by such economists as Jagdish Bhagwati of Columbia University, Paul Krugman of Stanford University, and Robert Lawrence of Harvard University.[59] It is consistent with empirical observations that point to an overall declining employment content of output (higher labour productivity) through time.

The problem is particularly acute for unskilled labour, which is more easily replaced by machines. At the beginning of the 1980s there was approximately 2 to 3 times as many unskilled workers as skilled workers looking for employment (1.9 in France, 2.2 in the United Kingdom, 3.1 in the United States). Ten years later this increased respectively to 3.5, 3.8, and 3.2. This excess unskilled work force has driven wages down in the United States and has created higher unemployment in the regulated European markets.[60]

Many economists believe, however, that in the long run labour markets will clear, that is, unskilled workers will consider education a profitable investment and will upgrade their skills, thus closing the gap documented above. Workers that have been shed in declining industries will find employment in the more dynamic sectors of the economy, which will receive a boost from the availability of such cheap labour. More importantly, the added productivity brought about by technological progress will increase incomes by making goods and services cheaper for consumers, thus sustaining demand for more goods and fueling growth.[61]

Empirical evidence, however, does not support such an optimistic outlook. Far from being a transitional phenomenon, the growth of joblessness and the erosion of real wages have been long-term trends since the 1970s. And the distortions of governmental policies cannot be blamed for thwarting the adjustments predicted by the theory—in fact both the European disease of rising joblessness, and the United States disease of low-quality, low-paid jobs, have accelerated since the beginning of the 1980s, precisely when most countries adopted free market reforms.[62]

Three structural changes in the global political economy
The current unemployment crisis is often compared with that of the 1930s, because of its severity. The only difference is that the 1930s had its theoretician, John Maynard Keynes, and its practitioner, United States President Franklin D. Roosevelt. In this age of open economies the economic profession is divided on how to diagnose the unemployment problem, and even more so on how to devise a cure. Hence the retrenchment to a microanalysis of labour markets. As suggested above, however, an analysis of the global employment crisis should go beyond the methodology of labour

market economics, to address the structural changes that have taken place in a multifaceted international economy—an economy in which multinational enterprises, states, and international organizations all interact to influence the rules of the game.

Indeed, analysts believe that the present world economy is conditioned by three interlocking structures, which define how states and firms operate: finance, production, and values or knowledge. Within each of these spheres the balance between states and markets shifts in response to changing norms, rules, or technological capabilities.[63] In each of these three areas interrelated changes have occurred, which have affected the ability of economies to create good jobs on a sustained basis.

A reordering of policy priorities. In asking ourselves "what has changed?" it is useful to look back at the "golden age" of full employment in the 1950s and 1960s and try and identify what made growth compatible, then, with employment and equity. In its *World Employment Report* the International Labour Organization (ILO) identifies three important features characteristic of the full employment period that reflect the three structures described above: the high priority given to employment in national and international policies, the social consensus over policies and institutions that would influence the distribution of income between profits and wages and maintain demand, and stable monetary and trading arrangements.[64]

The first factor followed a widespread perception that World War II was rooted in the frustration and economic dislocation of the Great Depression. Consequently, in the immediate postwar years most regimes in both the North and the South were highly interventionist. Likewise, employment figured prominently in the mandates given to the newly created international institutions—the World Bank, the IMF, the GATT or the UN.[65] By contrast, the protracted unemployment crisis of the 1970s and 1980s has been accompanied by an increasing acknowledgement that the problem is here to stay. Estimates of the natural rate of unemployment, or frictional unemployment, which encapsulates the effects of people moving in and out of work, have been raised steadily, from 2% to 6%. This figure constitutes the floor below which unemployment is not considered a problem warranting a policy effort, or below which policy efforts are deemed too costly in terms of inflation. Even though there is no firm empirical basis for establishing or calculating such a floor (the notion of non-inflation accelerating rate of unemployment is contested), this approach reveals the more general perception that ever higher levels of unemployment are acceptable, indeed unavoidable. This change is important because it indicates that policy priorities, rather than irrepressible forces of globalization, are at work.

The second group of factors—the breakdown in collective bargaining, the legitimacy crisis encountered by trade unions, and the dismantlement of the welfare state—has often been cited as an explanation for the growing inequality and in some cases falling real incomes observed in the West and in most developing countries (figure 3.4).

The decline in union membership has undoubtedly contributed to the stagnation or decline of real wages and, together with the decline of the welfare state, has contributed to the increased dispersion of income.

Nevertheless, even though the fight against inflation has taken precedence over the fight against unemployment in the last fifteen years, the unemployment dilemma seems to be a result of more than deliberate political choice (or lack thereof). Politicians feel that being able to deliver on the unemployment front is key to being elected, and opinion polls have shown

Figure 3.4 Union membership[a] as percentage of the labour force, Japan, United States and Western Europe,[b] 1970–93

(per cent)

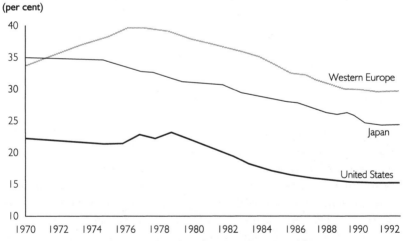

a. Annual union membership figures are adjusted to exclude retired members and retain employed members.
b. Western Europe includes France, Germany, Italy and the United Kingdom.
Source: UN/DESIPA, based on data from the United States Bureau of Labor Statistics, Division of Foreign Labor Statistics.

26

that unemployment, or job uncertainty, are often primary concerns of the electorate.

In this context the breakdown in collective bargaining, the legitimacy crisis encountered by trade unions, and the dismantling of the welfare state, cited by the ILO report, are a consequence rather than a cause of the policy impasse that has led governments to deregulate labour markets and phase out measures intended to promote human security.

Enhanced competition between states and between firms. When focusing on the environment in which economic actors operate, it appears that two sets of incentives are at work to nullify the self-clearing mechanisms of the market described earlier: across all sectors of the economy, firms have incentives to shed labour, and states have incentives to curb consumer demand.

Indeed, both states and firms condition economic outcomes. In deciding which lines of business to pursue; how, where and when to invest; and what mix of capital and labour to use, firms control the allocation of vast amounts of capital and human resources. States, in structuring the regulatory environment in which firms operate, determining subsidies to bestow on specific firms or sectors, or managing the national economy, also have an important, though arguably decreasing, role to play in outcomes such as global unemployment.

The incentive for firms to shed labour or curb wages originates in a cost-cutting drive necessitated by enhanced worldwide competition. In the race to lower costs of production some firms relocate labour-intensive activities abroad, encouraged by an ever more propitious investment climate in the South. These firms relocate production to lower-wage areas when the home country moves up the technological ladder and higher incomes, higher taxes, or unionization create upward pressure on wages. For example, manufacturing investment is moving from a first generation of Asian dragons, such as Singapore or Taiwan, to a second generation, such as Malaysia, the Philippines or Thailand.[66]

The availability of new technologies encourages other cost-cutting strategies, such as the relocation of activities in highly skilled markets. For example, some garment production is now done by skilled workers using computers and lasers that are programmed to cut fabric according to the pattern required. Thus international trade and technology are compatible, indeed complementary causes of the unemployment problem: the competitive pressure of low-wage countries creates an urgent need for firms to move into production processes that have a higher technological content. A competitive race between labour and capital as inputs in the production process fuels the move towards lower-wage areas.

Unfortunately, technological progress strengthens the case for capital in choosing inputs to production, especially if labour is unwilling to enter the competitive race with technology by accepting lower wages and benefits. In this respect, and all other things being equal, we are faced with mechanisms that could decrease the demand for labour, at current prices, with one exception: the use of complex machinery increases the demand for skilled labour, and thus its remuneration. Hence we see the growing wage dispersion between skilled and unskilled workers.

Data on the remuneration of labour confirms this analysis. Regardless of the distribution of wage earnings, the remuneration of labour has failed to keep pace with the remuneration of capital. In the 1980s the average real rate of return on investment in the United States was 4.3%. Between 1990 and 1994, this rate averaged 5.7% (a 25% gain), despite the recession of 1990–91.[67] At the same time, nominal wages and benefits in the United States have declined steadily since the early 1980s (figure 3.5). In addition, during the fiscal year that ended on March 31, 1995, the average worker's wage dropped 2.3% in real terms.[68]

Lower labour costs and higher profits are evidence of successful cost-cutting strategies. This success has led some observers to suspect that wage rates may not follow the progress of productivity—in other words, that higher

Figure 3.5 Employment cost index: changes in wages and salaries and benefit costs in private industry

(12-month percent change)

Source: United States Bureau of Labor.

productivity will not be passed on to workers in the form of higher wages.[69] Between 1977 and 1986 hourly earnings increased by up to three times as fast as productivity in industrial countries. Between 1992 and 1995, however, the rate of hourly wage growth was only 1.3 times that of productivity growth. In low- and middle-income countries earnings rose much faster than productivity in the 1970s. In the 1980s and the 1990s, however, half the countries that experienced a productivity increase experienced a smaller increase in earnings and, in some cases, no increase in earnings.[70] Figure 3.6 illustrates the wage/productivity gap in the case of the United States.

This pattern contradicts what would be expected in a free market, that the equilibrium level of wages equals the marginal productivity of labour. It is arguable, though, that in many countries where high unemployment prevails, employers enjoy quasi-monopoly power in the labour market and can therefore pay labour at less than the value of its marginal output, without being undercut by other employers competing for the same workers.[71] This behaviour is all the more likely in the new context of low unionization.

Aside from the discrepancy between global firms and national policy-making described above, there are many ways in which global competition changes outcomes in labour markets. For example, it has long been thought that nominal wages were inflexible downwards because employers felt that cutting pay checks of existing employees would damage morale and productivity. Yet, this unwritten taboo is receding because of the changing nature of labour markets: more and more jobs are high-turnover, fixed-term, part-time positions, in which workers have little contact with each

Figure 3.6 Productivity and pay

Index 1982 = 100

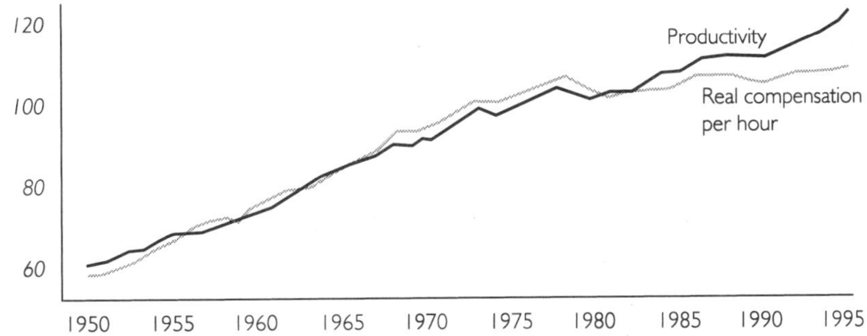

Source: Morgan Stanley.

29

other and do not think of their jobs as careers. In this context reducing the quantity of labour used and its remuneration, is easier.[72] This new, downwards flexibility of nominal wages stems from regulatory changes (allowing for fixed-term, part-time contracts) and, more fundamentally, from the high *firm* turnover brought about by increased competition.

In short, freer trade, freer global movement of capital (enhanced foreign direct investment), and technological advances have produced an environment that makes cost-cutting strategies easier to accomplish and more necessary for the individual firm. Yet, there is also a case for saying that individual firms benefit from the competitive slide of employment and wages, which, by depressing wage levels and creating a reserve army of unemployed, considerably improves their freedom of action in cutting costs, especially when weak aggregate demand at home may be offset by export opportunities. The fact that there seems to have been a trade-off between profits and wage costs since the early 1980s, at least in the United States, supports this view. In the words of one industrialist quoted in the *Wall Street Journal*, "Profits and balance sheets of corporate America are the best they have been since the 1960s . . . We have to believe that somewhere down the line working America will get its share".[73] But the record of the past 15 years shows that these good wishes are likely to remain immaterial given the powerful forces of globalization.

Gains in productivity, even if they are not passed on entirely to workers in the form of higher wages, should benefit workers to the extent that goods become cheaper—that their real incomes grow. But the demand boost produced by these real income gains is being undermined by policies that consistently thwart the global rise in real incomes.

There is at present a perverse incentive structure whereby nations feel that they will be better off if domestic demand is suppressed. Although all act according to what they feel is their own best interest, the outcome is that we are witnessing a global shortfall in demand for goods and services, which further depresses global output and employment.

In the present world economy all countries play a similar game: all vie for world market shares. Indeed, some authors have argued that the competition for market shares has supplanted the competition for territory.[74] What are the rules of this game and what are its costs and rewards?

Nations believe that the capture of market shares is the best way to increase their economic well-being. Competitiveness, which is measured by world market share for a particular product (and indirectly by the balance of trade), ensures that sales and profits will accrue to the firms based in a particular country. Likewise, nations are wary of seeing their domestic demand "leak abroad".

Both of these goals (conquering external markets, controlling the domestic market) can be achieved directly by using trade policies, for example, by subsidizing exports or by setting up tariffs and other barriers to protect the domestic market. But outright protectionism is frowned upon and is increasingly being constrained by strong international regimes.

Therefore, states are now resorting to nonprotectionist means of enhancing their competitiveness. The problem is that many of these policies entail curbing consumer demand at home.

For example, the quest for market share means that countries will find merit in policies aimed at boosting exports. Export promotion is a key component of the policy advice given to developing countries as part of structural adjustment programmes. This emphasis means that the conduct of economic affairs is geared towards serving foreign, not domestic markets; domestic demand is thus curbed—which is one of the reasons why structural adjustment programmes implemented worldwide are self-defeating.

Macroeconomic policy offers many opportunities to get an edge in world markets by curbing consumption at home. Through fiscal or monetary measures, aggregate demand can be manipulated, often in a countercyclical way—by slowing down an economy that threatens to overheat (and produce inflation) or by stimulating an economy that threatens to go into a recession. In practice, however, governments are now almost completely barred from stimulating their own economies in an effort to reduce unemployment, because in an open economy consumers with extra purchasing power will spend at least part of their new wealth on foreign goods, thus contributing to a deterioration of the balance of trade and of confidence in the domestic currency (and a potential currency crisis and investors' flight). The ease with which capital travels is undoubtedly a factor in this constraint. Enhanced domestic demand will also boost prices, which will make domestic goods less competitive abroad. In fact, a country in search of competitiveness has a clear incentive to maintain depressed demand at home.

Exchange rate policies also conspire to curb demand. In order for goods to be more competitive abroad, it is useful to keep the domestic currency undervalued. The methods for doing so depend on a country's exchange rate regime. If the dollar is low for example, United States cars will appear cheaper in foreign markets than their competitors. By the same token, imports are penalized when a currency is undervalued. Once more, consumer demand suffers, this time because more expensive foreign goods reduces real incomes.

Labour market policies geared towards more flexibility are being increasingly used as a way to reduce labour costs and improve a country's competitiveness in world markets. Ironically, however, labour market deregulation tends to depress aggregate demand by shifting income from wage earners, who spend a relatively high proportion of their income, towards earners of capital income, but without stimulating additional investment.[75]

Other policies are used by firms and governments to curb domestic demand. In Germany, for example, laws forbid stores from opening on Saturday afternoons and Sundays—with less time to shop, consumers will not only refrain from buying foreign goods, they will save more, thereby providing cheaper capital, which will make domestic firms more competitive. In Japan firms deliberately use pricing policies to gain advantages in foreign markets: they charge high prices to domestic consumers, and the proceeds allow them to charge lower prices in foreign markets. Again, domestic demand suffers.

Hence it is apparent that the short- or medium-term trends identified above are in fact part of a broader set of constraints and incentives in which both workers and consumers lose. In order to protect their future incomes, all countries vie for the position of being a producer but not a consumer. Clearly, these goals are incompatible, resulting in a zero-sum game. The aggregate effect of competition for market share results in insufficient demand for goods and services worldwide. As each country acts to curb its own domestic consumption, global demand fails to grow adequately, making everyone worse off—a typical case of Prisoner's Dilemma.

This shrinkage, in turn, creates employment-adverse incentives for firms. In a context of sluggish demand and increased competition, firms can only maintain profits by cutting costs and shedding labour, rather than by expanding production. Similarly, the excess labour that is pared down in restructuring efforts cannot find employment in the most dynamic sectors of the economy—as was the case historically—because even these sectors have to operate within stagnant markets.

As a result the growth of business investment or real capital formation has declined in OECD countries since the 1960s, and especially since the 1970s (table 3.1).

Traditionally, the shortfall in global demand has been seen as good insurance against inflationary pressures. But the sacrifice in terms of employment is beginning to cause alarm. For example, in its 1994 Annual Report the Bank for International Settlements (BIS) noted that "in order to actually reduce unemployment, [supply-side measures] need to be complemented by policies that allow aggregate demand to grow at a pace sufficient to gradually absorb cyclical and other sources of slack."[76]

The global demand shortfall is in fact an emerging issue—one that is usually limited to passing references, but never thoroughly analysed. As the 1995 UNCTAD Report indicates, "Neither the OECD study nor other studies of the causes of high unemployment give enough credit to demand factors and the policies shaping them."[77]

In order to understand these mechanisms, one must go beyond the conception of demand as a short-term variable and the belief that only supply issues are structural. It is, in fact, the long-standing structure of incentives for both states and firms that allows the world economy to function below its full employment frontier, thus preventing trade and technology from having their expected expansionary effects.

This pattern of employment-adverse incentives also stems from changes in the structure of capital markets and the context in which monetary policy is conducted.

Changes in the monetary system and in capital markets. Both states and firms have had to adjust to a new feature of the last 15 years—the rise in real inter-

Table 3.1 Real gross fixed capital formation in OECD countries
(average annual percentage increase)

	1960–68	1968–73	1973–79	1979–90
United States	5.0	3.7	1.9	2.5
Japan	15.2	12.2	1.6	5.0
European Union	6.0	5.0	0.1	2.5
Germany	3.1	5.4	0.4	1.9
France	8.0	6.8	0.1	2.3
United Kingdom	6.3	2.0	0.2	3.2
Total OECD	6.5	5.8	1.1	3.1

Source: UNCTAD 1995, calculated from *OECD Historical Statistics 1960–1990*. Paris: OECD 1992. These figures are in line with those on real gross domestic fixed investment provided by the World Bank, *World Data 1994* (on CD-ROM).

est rates, particularly long-term ones. Higher real interest rates have meant that the value of debt has soared (table 3.2). In order to reduce indebtedness, firms have had to cut costs and restructure their production processes, thus shedding labour. States have had to cut back on social services and public investment, with direct and indirect negative consequences on employment, training, and private investment.

Apart from the financial pressure that they generate among firms, high interest rates are detrimental to employment because they hurt private investment. This direct effect is probably less salient in developing countries, where investment depends on a wider set of factors. Yet, in most cases higher interest rates will make borrowing, and therefore investment, more costly. In fact, productive investment will only be undertaken if its expected yield is higher than that which money markets can offer. Thus in many cases large companies would sooner invest their profits in remunerative capital markets rather than reinvest them in their own lines of business.

Higher interest rates also hurt employment through pricing mechanisms. In a competitive environment firms usually have a choice of keep-

Table 3.2 Long-term real interest rates in major industrialized countries: a historical comparison

(percentage)

Country	1890–1899	1900–1913	1924–1929	1930–1932	1933–1939	1956–1973	1974–1980	1981–1993
United States	5.4	2.3	3.6	11.5	1.1	1.1	−0.3	5.6
Canada	—	1.6	4.9	10.0	1.8	2.2	0.3	6.7
Japan	—	—	—	—	—	0.3	0.5	4.4
Germany	2.9	3.5	5.3	17.1	4.9	3.0	3.0	4.5
France	3.8	1.8	0.2	7.1	−1.2	1.0	0.4	5.7
United Kingdom	1.9	2.7	5.5	6.4	2.1	1.8	−3.3	4.5
Italy	—	—	5.7	12.7	0.4	1.1	−5.0	4.2
Average of four countries (US, UK, Germany, France)	3.5	2.6	3.7	10.5	1.7	1.7	0.0	5.1

Source: Robert Rowthorn, "Capital Formation and Unemployment". *Oxford Review of Economic Policy.* 2(1). 1995. Reproduced from UNCTAD 1995.

ing prices low while increasing market shares, or charging high prices and collecting higher profits immediately, but at the expense of market shares (and future profits). If they follow the first strategy, they will sell and produce more goods and services now, thereby employing more workers. If they chose the latter strategy, their profits will come mainly from charging more for the same quantity of goods (hence they have less need for workers).

If the interest rate is high, waiting for future profits becomes expensive—any revenue collected now could earn high interest. Hence firms are inclined to charge higher prices now (higher markups), even if production does not grow in volume. And stagnating volumes mean higher unemployment.[78]

High interest rates also affect firms through their effects on states. The retrenchment of public investment, due to higher interest rates, has had negative consequences for private investment, because public investment in infrastructure encourages private investment by making it more profitable. It has been calculated that each percentage point increase in public investment is associated with a 0.4–0.6 percentage point increase in private investment in equipment.[79]

Finally, high or volatile interest rates also affect the demand side of the economy in ways that go beyond its well-known effects on customer borrowing.

Interest rate volatility in the past twenty years is illustrated by the example of the British pound.

Wide fluctuations in interest rates affects consumer expenditure by changing the value of household wealth, notably in real estate, and the value of consumer debt—all of which affect the amount of money that will be spent on consuming goods and services. In France, Germany, Japan, and the United States, the volatility of real consumption expenditure from 1961–73 to 1982–94 increased from 78% to 167%. In fact, income volatility has increased for all consumers, whether asset holders or workers. For workers, this is due to the growing number of fixed-term, part-time, high-turnover jobs. Unstable expectations of future income, whether from work or from savings, tend to dampen consumption.

In addition, the volatility of domestic demand has been accompanied by the increased volatility of demand in foreign markets, as a result of currency fluctuations. The volatility of real exports and imports, which are also components of aggregate demand, increased four-fold on average. As a result of this uncertainty there has been a significant slowdown in investment, reflected in a decline in capital formation.[80] All this movement has increased the risk for firms of investing in expanding production, and thereby hiring labour.[81]

Why has there been a trend towards higher and more volatile real interest rates in the last fifteen to twenty years? The cause can be found in the structure of capital markets and in the policies pursued by states. Innovations in capital markets—such as derivatives—have provided high-yielding alternatives to investors, thus putting upwards pressure on real interest rates. When the yield offered by simple bonds and notes are too low, investors have the option of buying more attractive and remunerative instruments, thus forcing an upward adjustment in both long-term and short-term interest rates.

Higher interest rates also result from the fact that, because of severe fiscal constraints, states have been more and more inclined to use monetary policy to fight inflation, conduct counter-cyclical policies, and offset the pressure on their exchange rates. The last illustrates the interdependent nature of all these phenomena. Because of openness in product markets, changes in demand (for example a cyclical upswing) will draw in goods from abroad and put pressure on the national currency. Deregulated financial markets will largely amplify the trend by taking speculative positions against that same currency. Because currency depreciation poses a risk of imported inflation, the typical response of governments will be to restore the attractiveness of the national currency by increasing its rate of interest.

This reactive use of short-term interest rates, in turn, negatively affects long-term rates, which typically reflect expectations of the future evolution of short-term rates, with a risk premium. High interest rate expectations result from the belief that central banks will use interest rates whenever the national currency is put under stress.

For states, higher interest rates have meant a growing debt burden. In the G-7 countries as a whole the burden of interest payment each year is almost as large as the budget deficit itself. This debt overhang has meant a curtailment of investment in human and material assets, as well as further currency volatility and pressure on the worldwide pool of savings.

In conclusion, we have seen that the global unemployment problem is structural rather than cyclical, and is largely due to a shortfall in the demand for labour. Superficially, the lower demand for workers is due to the effects of technological progress, and in the North, to competition from low-wage economies. In theory, however, neither international trade nor technology should lead to a net decrease in global employment, and historically this has not been the case. Instead, several changes in the current global economy are responsible for this unexpected outcome: increased competition between states, which thwarts global demand growth; increased competition between firms in the context of a fragmented global political order, which maintains low incomes and labour standards; a spiral of high interest rates and state indebtedness, in part due to deregulated financial markets; and a declining commitment to full employment.

4.
Review of Policy Options

Policy-making in this complex and interdependent environment is, needless to say, difficult, especially if one intends to take full advantage of the wealth-creating effect of markets, while ensuring that workers do not bear the burden of adjustments. Too often, policy prescriptions do not acknowledge the problem of trade-offs. For example, policy-makers are advised to keep inflation low and maintain small budget deficits (all encapsulated in the code word "sound" domestic policies), yet at the same time provide effective social safety nets and universal, high-quality education.[82] This section will attempt to highlight existing policy trade-offs and suggest ways of moving beyond these trade-offs.

A complete range of policy options would include measures targeted at the labour market but also, more broadly, measures that address the decreased demand for labour, whether in relation to macroeconomic variables (such as growth or aggregate demand) or to microeconomic variables (such as investment and hiring).

Policy-making also needs to acknowledge specific situations, as well as local needs, habits, and preferences. Lack of formal employment may endanger the stability of societies to different degrees, as exemplified above. Likewise, opinion polls have shown that the public may have a higher or lower tolerance for income inequality across cultures and countries. Again, citizens should be the ultimate arbiters when choices between societal values need to be made, for example, between equality and wealth creation. Local preferences can also affect how effective policy proposals, such as "workfare", or "work-sharing", are. Therefore, in unemployment as in other areas, a good rule of thumb is that decisions should be made by subsidiarity, that is, at the lowest practical political level. The particular challenge that confronts national policy-makers is that the threshold at which policy action loses its efficiency is constantly moving upwards, beyond the borders of the nation-state. Yet, even though the scope for policies at the national level has shrunk considerably, national policy-makers need to take up the challenge and explore what opportunities remain for boosting employment in an integrating world economy.

In both the national and the international sphere the same problem applies: How does one adjust production and consumption? How does one "reveal" the latent demand for goods (demand of those who have no purchasing power), and translate it into a higher demand for labour?

AT THE NATIONAL LEVEL

Adjusting the supply of, and demand for, labour
Governments can help to match supply and demand, for example, by providing education and other services. Governments can also help employees and employers find arrangements that are mutually suitable and that promote larger societal goals.

The role of labour market policies. As noted earlier, a large proportion of labour analysts view the unemployment problem (especially that of Europe and Latin America) as a by-product of inefficient labour markets—markets that have been distorted by governmental regulations or by wage-setting practices. The European White Paper on Growth, Competitiveness, and Employment calls for greater flexibility in the labour market and an examination of social protection systems to ensure that they encourage people to work.[83]

Deregulation of labour markets, however, poses theoretical and practical difficulties. Empirically, the link between labour market rules and unemployment is contested.[84] Paul Krugman, for example, asks in a recent article why, if this assumption is true, the United States experienced a much higher rate of unemployment than Europe throughout the 1970s.[85] There does not seem to be a correlation over time between increased labour market flexibility and increased employment.[86] Labour markets have, in fact, become much more flexible in the past ten years, without an overall improvement in employment.[87] In a systematic comparison of Spain and Portugal, Olivier Blanchard and Juan F. Jimeno found that, even though Spain had the highest unemployment rate in the European Union (24.4%) and Portugal has the second lowest (6.8%), labour market institutions were remarkably similar in the two countries—probably more similar than any other pair of European countries.[88]

Moreover, the theoretical case for nonintervention in labour markets is not clear. In particular, the belief that employers enjoy monopoly power is widely held to justify measures such as the minimum wage.[89] As mentioned above, labour market deregulation may improve the competitive position of a particular firm or country, but when enacted by all participants in the international system, it undermines employment by depressing demand.

On the practical side an erosion of labour standards is likely to lead to a widening income spread and possibly to greater real poverty, as the downward pressure on wages, rights, and benefits will hit the most vulnerable members of society.

Nevertheless, labour market adjustments are useful when they do not produce income volatility or uncertainty. The broader goal of matching supply and demand at various skill levels is important and can be furthered with measures such as worker relocation and retraining, the efficient distribution of information and a regulatory environment that provides adequate incentives and protects both employers and employees. Of particular interest is the provision of education services for the unemployed.

The role of training and education. Calls for enhancing training and education flow from the observation that there are labour shortages in new, dynamic sectors of the economy that require specific skills. An improved training system would help match supply and demand, and in general would create a better-educated and more adaptable work force.[90]

Public investment in education benefits both employees and employers—employees for obvious reasons and employers because they are less pressured to provide compensation sufficient to cover their employees' past educational costs. It also brings additional benefits in terms of human development and equal opportunity to participate in the political, economic and cultural life of a nation.

Education and training, however, seem to be necessary, not sufficient conditions for better employment performance. In developing countries strong state investment in universal education has yielded very high returns. It has allowed countries such as Taiwan and Republic of Korea to move into more technologically advanced sectors and reap higher value-added. In Western Europe, however, many young people delay their entry into the work force by studying longer, resulting in a glut of highly trained graduates. In Germany, for example, 43% of the unemployed have passed through the country's renowned apprenticeship system.[91]

Work-sharing. Beyond facilitating labour market adjustments, the idea of reducing work hours in order to increase the number of people at work has been revived in the last decade by both states and firms. In firm-based arrangements workers typically trade shorter working hours and less-than-proportional pay cuts for more work time flexibility, which allows the company to operate shifts and thus maximize the use of capital assets.

In November 1993, for example, Volkswagen AG, Europe's largest auto manufacturer, reached an agreement with the German IG Metall union to put more than 100,000 workers on a 29-hour, four-day week, while cutting their pay by nearly 10%. Similar schemes have been put into effect by Hewlett Packard in France, Coopers and Lybrand in New York and the First Chicago Bank.[92] In France a bill for reducing the standard work week to 32 hours, down from 39, accompanied by a 3–8% wage cut and supported by tax incentives, passed the Senate in October 1993, although it failed to pass the National Assembly.

Work-sharing is in keeping with the historical trend towards shorter work hours—from a typical 12-hour work day in the 19th century, to 10 hours, then 8 hours—which has been accompanied by a steady rise in productivity. In the United States, for example, if the national workload were shared equally among all adults, each would have to work two-and-a-half hours a day.[93]

This long-term trend reflects the learning capacity of societies, and recent studies have proved its wisdom. For example, studies have found that in countries in which long hours are the norm, workers are more likely to be dissatisfied with their jobs and with their employers.[94] There is mounting evidence that the competitive pressure on workers from the threat of unemployment leads to ever longer hours, with detrimental effects on mental and physical health. A Californian study has shown that those working more than 48 hours a week have twice the risk of dying from heart disease as those working 40 hours or less. Long work hours are an important factor in occupational stress, which is estimated to cost the United Kingdom $4.6 billion a year.[95]

Working less can also allow people to participate in community life through volunteer activities, non-governmental organizations or political activism, and in family life, by better sharing household responsibilities and allowing for more bonding time with friends, children and spouses. Political participation and social and gender equity would be boosted, resulting in greater social and family stability.[96]

Conceived as a ongoing process rather than as a one-time fix, work-sharing may mitigate the long-term effects of productivity gains, which at present seem to be creating a class of burnt-out workers and a growing class of idle, marginalized unemployed.

Although shorter work hours raise hourly productivity, work-sharing schemes may not make economic sense to all firms because there are a number of fixed costs (administrative costs, benefits and so on) that remain to be borne for each employee. Employers are especially wary of regulations mandating such changes in the work place, although they welcome the rise of part-time work when it is accompanied by reduced benefits.[97]

If a common, nation-wide change in standard work hours is not politically or economically feasible, selected incentives can be provided to firms that are willing to create more jobs by spreading the workload. Beyond these incentives, a culture of work-sharing could be promoted, for example, by developing comanagement techniques, using innovative software. The barriers to entry into the job market constituted by fixed health costs could be alleviated by gradually disconnecting health coverage and employment.

Sharing the work load, however, will probably not expand overall labour demand in an economy. Hence it is important to facilitate a dynamic cycle of higher production, income, and revenue.

Encouraging productive investment
A key component in closing the gap between production and consumption lies in the way investment is conducted. Investors are essential economic actors in that they identify a potential demand for a good or service and arrange for this good or service to be produced, thereby hiring workers.

Many obstacles may interfere with this virtuous, employment-creating process, however.

Promoting an environment conducive to investment. Investors make decisions based on their calculations of how demand will evolve in particular sectors, how expensive it will be to produce the particular good or service (depending on the future price of inputs), how much tax they can be expected to pay, and so on. Hence the biggest enemy of an investor is uncertainty. And, conversely, predictability constitutes the most propitious environment for investment. It is no wonder that country risk analysis has become such an important component of private investment in developing countries.

Countries that seek to promote investment should therefore strive to provide continuity and predictability in their economic policies, even though this goal may conflict, at times, with the necessity of being responsive to citizens' needs and the outcomes of periodic elections.

For example, the rules that govern trade or taxes should not be changed too frequently, regardless of their content. In the context of developing and transition economies, the key is to provide and enforce a legal framework for economic activities—property rights, recourse in the case of bankruptcy or insolvency, protection against racket and fraud, and so on—as well as efficient transport and communication infrastructure. In order to close the gap between cash-starved economies and the growing volume of international money looking for remunerative investment, institutions that will provide clear rules and enforce fair practices for the exchange of bonds and securities must be created. The case of Russia, for example, is yet another reminder that strong institutions are needed in order to take advantage of market efficiency.[98]

The successful experiences of South-East Asian countries also point to the importance of tapping domestic sources of capital, by encouraging private savings or restricting capital exports.[99]

A stable currency is also an important asset, especially for attracting inwards investment. Indeed, investors are loath to buy securities denominated in a currency that will depreciate. Maintaining a stable currency is often understood to mean enacting restrictive policies—hence the deflationary ring of the expression stabilization policies. Yet, balanced budgets are only one way to promote stable currencies: uncertainty may be contained, for example, by creating a single currency zone with major trading partners. This is one example in which regional solutions may offer more immediately feasible alternatives to global solutions.

Too often, the understanding of what constitutes a predictable environment for investment has been restricted to mean balanced budgets and the attendant fiscal austerity. In fact, legal, social and environmental components are equally important, as witnessed by the intense interest of investors in more country-specific information on these indicators.[100]

Making taxes more "employment-friendly". In many countries employers are faced with heavy non-wage costs, which reduce the incentive to hire workers and end up making production processes with a high capital content all the more attractive. Therefore, governments are more and more inclined to lighten the loads of employers by reducing payroll taxes and turning the bill over to other taxpayers.

In France, for example, health insurance, which used to be financed exclusively by workers and their employers, is now partly financed from the general budget through an additional tax on all sources of income, the Generalized Social Contribution. Recently, a reduction in the duties payable by employers has been enacted. It will be financed by an increase in the rate of the value-added tax. Five European countries—Denmark, Finland, the Netherlands, Norway and, Sweden—are implementing a tax on polluting activities (such as household consumption of energy), often with the explicit goal of shifting taxation away from employment. The Labour Party in the United Kingdom is also considering such a levy.[101]

Ensuring sustainable demand growth. In industrial, developing, and transition economies job losses have resulted from policies that focused on other goals at the expense of employment and demand growth. These policies should be seriously reconsidered or reformulated with a view to reducing their costs in terms of employment.

In Western Europe the convergence criteria mandated by the Maastricht Treaty, if retained, will further exacerbate the contractionary effects of the EMS. Countries such as the United Kingdom, which have allowed their currencies to leave the EMS, have been rewarded in terms of job creation. Indeed, since the British pound left the EMS in 1992, the British economy experienced steady employment growth, by more than 630,000 by March 1995, bringing the unemployment rate down to 8.4%—a performance unique in the European Union.[102]

Conversely, as we have seen, if individual countries of the European Union implement the contractionary convergence criteria, it may cost them an estimated 1.0 to 1.5 million jobs. The experience of Spain shows that the costly efforts (in human terms) of reducing social security benefits have been wiped out within a few years by recession and tight monetary policies aimed at keeping the peseta inside the EMS.[103]

The ultimate goal of a single European currency is nonetheless a positive step for employment. But in light of the high interim costs, an alternative strategy for transition should be envisaged. This is important especially because a hysteresis effect is often at work, whereby unemployed people risk becoming permanently unemployable, thus creating a pool of long-term marginalized workers and making the unemployment problem very difficult to reverse.

Indeed, the hysteresis effect could add an element of irreversibility to the problem of unemployment.[104] It would not seem reasonable, therefore, to sacrifice the future of a whole generation for the sake of offering security to current asset holders. Once again, the imperative of human development should stimulate the formulation of alternative scenarios.

In transition economies, on the other hand, the contractionary effects of liberalization measures arose because supply conditions were not in place when prices were liberalized. Hence runaway inflation occurred, reducing real earnings, depressing demand, and producing mass unemployment.[105] The pace and ranking of liberalization measures should therefore be reexamined, with a view to providing the legal and industrial environment conducive to a dynamic private sector.

In some developing countries policies for macroeconomic stabilization and structural adjustment have curbed demand by raising the prices of basic commodities and utilities, reducing state spending, restricting money supply and credit, increasing real interest rates and encouraging state-owned and other firms to lay off workers. The effect has often been contractionary. Hence even though in theory firms had a better environment in which to invest, investment lagged because these policies that enhanced the investment climate reduced the living standards and purchasing power of the local people. These perverse effects need to be addressed, and policies should be implemented, along the lines suggested above, to boost investment without simultaneously curbing aggregate demand.[106]

Promoting the efficient flow of money and credit. Sometimes the quantity of investment is less of an issue than is the kind of investment, where it flows to, how it is managed, and who benefits from it. For example, inwards portfolio investment to developing countries can raise the exchange rate of a country's currency, thereby harming its export prospects. And since a correlation has been found in most developing countries between wage growth and export orientation, excessive inwards investment resulting in an appreciating exchange rate may have adverse effects on industrial activity, employment and wages.[107] Strategies to mitigate this undesirable effect and encourage foreign direct investment, while discouraging the more speculative short-term loans or portfolio investments, have proved relatively successful in countries that have implemented them, and have recently been endorsed by the IMF.[108]

In addition, developing countries can make the most of foreign direct investment provided that, for the larger projects, the terms of investment are carefully negotiated with a view to the future—ensuring that they include technology transfers or encourage spillover effects on local suppliers.[109] Conversely, the scramble for investment that leads developing countries to compete with ever higher tax incentives or to waive labour and safety standards is clearly counter-productive. As will be explained later on, this is one area in which domestic action is constrained and in which there is scope for international initiatives.

The distribution of money and credit inside an economy may also have considerable consequences on employment performance. Most employment growth occurs in small and medium-sized firms. Yet, those businesses encounter the most difficulty in obtaining credit. Therefore micro-banking and lending to the poor are very effective strategies to reduce unemployment and promote self-employment, particularly in economies in which the formal sector cannot be relied on to generate enough jobs. In addition, small loans are most effective at reducing poverty and improving the participation of women in economic activity. The success of the Grameen Bank in Bangladesh has recently prompted the World Bank to earmark $200 million in small loans to individuals. These efforts should be amplified and broadened, and be framed within a more general policy of support for the informal and small-farm sectors in which the majority of developing-country workers are currently employed.[110]

Revealing the latent demand for labour

A mismatch between production and consumption may occur because the demand for goods and services is not translated into supply. Several factors may account for this outcome. First, this demand may remain unexpressed because those who need the goods and services cannot afford to pay for them. Second, these services may be public goods, and therefore market incentives are not great enough for entrepreneurs to undertake their production.[111]

Promoting the employment of labour in services. Services are the fastest-growing sector in terms of employment creation worldwide (table 4.1).

Growth areas include services to businesses, such as financial and legal counseling, for which industrial countries now have a comparative advantage, and personal services, which include social services and range from domestic help and care for the aged and the young, to health, education, training, and the provision of sports and cultural opportunities. As John Langmore and John Quiggin have noted, these community-oriented services have experienced retrenchment everywhere and have suffered from cutbacks in state spending, simultaneously increasing the number of people looking for employment and the number needing the services. Therefore a serious effort to expand publicly financed community services should be undertaken.[112] Subsidizing such employment opportunities should alleviate the solvency problem faced by those who need the services.

Sceptics may ask, however, why public authorities should subsidize the provision of services to private individuals. Why is it that the market cannot

Table 4.1 Structure of world employment, 1965 and 1989–91

	Agriculture		Industry		Services	
	1965	1989–91	1965	1989–91	1965	1989–91
World	57	48	19	17	24	35
Industrial countries	22	7	37	26	41	67
Developing countries	72	61	11	14	17	25
East and South-East Asia	73	50	9	18	18	32
Sub-Saharan Africa	79	67	8	9	13	24

Note: For East and South-East Asia figures are for 1960; industry includes only manufacturing.
Source: ILO, labour statistics on diskette (Geneva, 1994).

provide social and personal services? Why not subsidize consumption for everyone instead?

The answer is threefold. First, services tend to be more labour-intensive than manufacturing or agriculture—hence, the amount of employment for every dollar (or zloti, or rand and so on) spent by public authorities will be higher.

Second, such subsidization helps to fulfil societal goals. For example, the goal of equal opportunity for women is advanced when public authorities subsidize child care; the goal of equal opportunity in general is furthered when education is made more affordable; the goal of human development is enhanced when more opportunities are open for people to develop and exercise their minds and bodies through cultural and recreational activities as they become freer from the daily struggles for health or livelihood. Furthermore, normative economic theory has long recognized that the marginal value of an additional dollar is higher when spent on the poor than on the rich. Therefore it is more efficient to subsidize services to disadvantaged groups.

Third, many social services have a public good component—they benefit not only their nominal recipients, but many members of society. A good example is crime prevention. John Langmore and John Quiggin note, for example, that the daunting social cost of family breakdown could be avoided if public authorities made marriage and family counseling more accessible and available. Likewise, prevention of child abuse has enormous future rewards in terms of crime prevention. More broadly, education and poverty alleviation contribute to creating a safer society for all citizens. "Green" jobs—that involve the monitoring and relief of threats to the environment—also benefit the entire community.

Building public infrastructure. Telecommunication and transport infrastructures improve a country's productivity and the rate of return of capital invested in that country. By facilitating business transactions and bringing intangible rewards to citizens in terms of convenience, they often largely repay the cost of their construction and maintenance. Hence public investment boosts private investment and employment. Again, these benefits have been overlooked and infrastructure has been allowed to deteriorate in many industrial and developing countries in the past 10 to 20 years. In Germany and the United Kingdom, for example, government real investment in fixed capital was 15% lower in 1990 than in 1972.[113]

The fact that building and maintaining transport infrastructure is labour intensive and that there is a latent demand for it, makes it a suitable sector for public investment. Likewise, programmes aimed at improving the channels of communications for goods, people, and information will bring employment, as well as larger economic benefits.

Public work programmes. Direct employment provided by public authorities is a very old idea, dating back to work programmes for the poor in Elizabethan England, to the Tennessee Valley Authority, to the pan-European infrastructure projects proposed by the European White Paper on Unemployment.

Economically, these schemes are justified by the fact that public goods (such as infrastructure, social stability, and law and order) are undersupplied by the market. The schemes aim to staff community projects with the excess labour that the private sector will not hire. Social stability is enhanced by providing a safety net and allowing the unemployed to reclaim participation in community life. In developing countries public work programmes are considered a useful tool to alleviate poverty, and have been used extensively in Costa Rica, India, Republic of Korea, and Sri Lanka.[114]

Work programme schemes have two drawbacks, however: they cost more in terms of organization and supervision than do hand-outs, and they require substantial funding, while their immediate benefits are less financially tangible or visible than private sector employment.

These objections are also true of other measures aimed at revealing the latent demand for labour. Their potential costs seem to contradict the aims of achieving macroeconomic stabilization and smaller budget deficits. Too much government spending and borrowing may also raise interest rates and absorb domestic savings that would otherwise go towards private investment. Levying the necessary financing for these programmes should not occur at the expense of private employment.

In this respect, some funding suggestions raise concern. Funding community employment by levying a value-added tax on high-technology goods and services is likely to curb the most dynamic (and therefore job-creating) sections of the economy. Likewise, discontinuing subsidies to multinational corporations, although a seemingly attractive proposition, may be harmful if the subsidies are being paid to sustain basic research and development (which have positive externalities) or are being paid as incentives for implementing socially desirable schemes (such as work-sharing).

And cutting welfare programmes may be risky in the absence of viable alternatives.[115]

Restoring the financial capacities of states. As explained above, fiscal constraints within states have worsened, creating a large debt overhang, even in industrial countries. For example, the gross debt of OECD economies has grown, from an average of 42% of GDP in 1980 to 71% in 1994. Interest payments on government debt have become a major source of spending for states, making the problem cumulative.

This burden hinders states' capacities to provide social safety nets, to act as employers of last resort, or to provide incentives of firms to employ certain types of workers or set up operations in depressed areas, without further endangering employment prospects by increasing taxes.

It also contributes to slower growth and investment, because the financial needs of states help to keep interest rates high and because the paralysis of fiscal policy means that monetary policy—especially interest rates—is the only instrument of macroeconomic management.

Why are states so indebted?
States' fiscal crises are due to slower growth, tight monetary policies, unemployment and its costs, and demographic changes that increase overall spending on pensions.

An additional, under-researched factor has been the revenue shortfalls brought about by the internationalization of firms. Multinational companies have managed to escape the taxation constraints faced by their domestic counterparts, by either changing the prices of goods traded among firm affiliates in order to post higher profits in low-tax countries (transfer pricing), or by playing one state against another in the global scramble for international investment. While the first phenomenon is especially prevalent in developing countries (in the form of tax holidays to attract foreign direct investment), the problem also exists, though in a slightly different form, in industrial countries where multinational companies are headquartered. For example, French tax authorities have estimated that fiscal integration, a favourable tax regime applied to major domestic multinational companies, amounted to a FF19 billion ($38 billion) shortfall for the Treasury—in addition to the foregone income arising from other comparable regimes and from practices such as transfer pricing.[116] This amount is comparable to the FF20 billion expected annual revenue from the "Contribution for Reimbursement of the Debt", a new across-the-board income tax designed to offset the deficit of the national health system and other welfare payment accounts (such as family allowances).

In addition, increased capital mobility and the phase-out of exchange controls have allowed savings to flee to low-tax countries. For example, the deduction at source levied by the German government on capital gains is increasingly being avoided by German banks, which are setting up affiliates in neighbouring Luxembourg.

In a way, then, the current fiscal crisis may be interpreted as resulting from the growing discrepancy between a global world economy and a political structure that remains fragmented among states.

The financing dilemma is just one area in which global policy is being called upon to replace national policy-making, as the latter has become less and less efficient. National investment policies are vulnerable to interest rates prevailing in the outside world. National demand management is vulnerable to the sanction of financial markets. And investment in infrastructure and social services is made difficult by the competitive lowering of tax rates, and hence the squeeze on fiscal revenue.

POLICIES AT THE INTERNATIONAL LEVEL

Breaking the world economy's bias against demand growth and employment

The need for coordinated action. We have seen that states are engaged in a competition for market shares that should be healthy and growth-promoting, but that is in fact a zero-sum game. If the growth of income that would normally follow from increased efficiency is being undermined by stagnant real wages or is being concentrated in the hands of a few, then states and firms will scramble for a demand pie that remains constant and may even shrink if cost-cutting, labour-saving measures reduce the aggregate income of workers, and if the attendant uncertainty reduces their propensity to spend.

The competitive game among states could thus lead to higher unemployment through a competitive reining in of consumer demand in each domestic economy. This outcome may also result from the difficulty most countries experience in managing demand in an open economy.

Indeed, the national measures described above—ensuring sustainable demand growth, public promotion of human and real investment—could contribute to growth and employment. But when implemented in isolation, these measures create distortions and unsustainable pressures on public finance and external balances. Even the United States is not immune from this external constraint. In the 1980s its expansionary policy and growing budget deficits resulted in a surge of imports and a deterioration in its external trade balance. In smaller countries this effect is being compounded by the fact that the accompanying currency depreciation must be reversed by raising interest rates.

If all major economies, however, agree to boost demand at the same time, trade patterns should not be significantly altered, and pressures on national currencies should be limited. A coordinated boost in demand and investment should therefore generate significant shared benefits, as many econometric studies have found.[117]

Presently, as former Labour Secretary Ray Marshall notes, "the absence of policy coordination—especially among the United States, Germany and Japan—hampers global growth and stability".[118]

Firms also have a stake in making sure that global demand is sustained. Ideally, firms would like to pay their employees as little as possible (in order to reduce costs), but would also like their competitors to pay their employees as much as possible (in order to sustain the aggregate demand for goods and services). In the 1920s the Ford car company was able to boost domestic demand (and therefore the demand for its own cars) by raising the wages of its own employees, because it was a major player in the overall American industrial landscape. Now, however, individual companies are neither willing nor able to improve aggregate demand through wage policies. Yet, overall, the vested interests firms have in growing markets is evident. This creates a typical case of collective action dilemma, hence the need for coordinated public action.

The scope for coordinated action. Coordinated policies have been agreed to in the late 1970s and in the 1980s among the Group of Seven countries.[119] They have fallen out of favour somewhat because every country is not necessarily at the same stage of the business cycle, and economic stimulation in countries that are experiencing an expansion may create inflation. Also, many countries want to stimulate their economies before scheduled elections, and "political cycles" do not necessarily match. Thus although there are common benefits, these benefits are not always equally divided. Firms may also have a shorter horizon, and may be more concerned with cutting costs now and more apprehensive about creating a wage-price spiral that could eat into their profits.

Clearly, a policy dialogue will be needed. The fact that gains will be unequal should not be a deterrent. After all, free trade and free markets also bring benefits that are unequally divided, yet this does not disqualify free-market policies in the minds of most decision-makers. It should be kept in mind that the alternative is a loss of economic control by nations locked in a vicious circle of low demand and stagnant production.

Numerous forums exist for such coordination, such as the OECD, the G-7, or the Interim Committee of the IMF. Experience shows that these measures are more politically sensitive than they appear to be, and decisions end up being taken at the highest levels of governments after a process of informal and often discrete negotiations. Hence there does not seem to be a justification for creating a new international body for the purpose. This is one instance in which norms and practices should change before institutions step in to solidify them. For example, coordination of monetary policies has shown a recent revival in the joint action by central banks to reverse the slide of the dollar.[120] The key factor will be citizens exerting pressure on their elected officials, demanding a solution to the unemployment problem.

Addressing competitive pressures against remunerative employment
The case for universal labour standards. In an anarchic international environment firms have an incentive to shop around the world in search for workers willing to put in the longest hours for the least pay. This behaviour is redolent of the classical theory according to which the equilibrium wage will converge around the subsistence income level. The term "willing workers", however, belongs more to the fiction of rational economic agents than to the reality of imperfect information and sunk costs. In many developing countries workers are lured by false promises of attractive wages and go into debt to pay for their journeys to a city or an export-processing zone where harsher conditions than expected await them.

It is now becoming apparent that failure to implement minimum labour standards in one country may hurt the workers concerned as well as all other workers in a labour market that is increasingly global. The competitive race to attract foreign direct investment creates a bias against the implementation of fair labour practices, at least in most developing countries. Hence there is a case for negotiating a floor on labour conditions worldwide. Stronger international rules for decent working conditions would level the playing field and prevent firms from gaining an edge in world markets by using unethical work practices, and simultaneously putting downward pressure on world wages.

The implementation of universal labour standards. There are rules against exploitative work at both the national and international levels. They should be strengthened and possibly backed by consumer initiatives, such as labels guaranteeing that the products have been manufactured under fair and humane conditions. The International Labour Organization could help to monitor eligible businesses. The experience of "voluntary" consumer pressure, however, has proved to be effective only when a brand name was at stake and when strong methods were used, for example, the threat of a boycott.[121]

The question of international labour standards, however, is controversial. Developing countries see it as a protectionist measure in disguise and as an attempt to erode their comparative advantage, which consists of lower labour costs. In order to address these objections, current discussions of international labour standards have ruled out notions of an international minimum wage, concentrating instead on the notion of worker's rights, embodying qualitative rights (such as a ban on child labour, or the right to organize), rather than wage levels.

The ultimate objective of international labour standards should not be to save low-skilled jobs in the North by "outlawing" cheaper labour in the South, but to act as a counterweight to the growing mobility of international capital. Developing countries also argue that low labour standards are prevalent in the non-export sector and that aid rather than trade measures would better address the problem.

To some extent, however, the debate is not simply a North-South issue, as industrial countries also could find international labour standards highly constraining. For example, the United States has not ratified ILO conventions 112 and 124, which pertain to certain aspects of the right of labour to organize—rights that are being considered for universal application.

One solution would be to promote these standards by encouraging trade unions and by enhancing development assistance, notably in education. Improving the bargaining power of the work force will also mean promoting responsive governance, law-enforcement capabilities, political participation and democratic processes in developing countries.

Cooperation in solving financial and monetary dilemmas

Addressing fiscal constraints within states. The scope for international solutions to the fiscal crisis experienced by states is large in theory, but this area of global policy-making is still in its infancy. For example, rules for the taxation of multinational enterprises have been negotiated in multilateral forums, with little success. The climate for a revival of such negotiations seems favourable, though, because the United States is currently revising its own rules, with the goal of ensuring that multinational enterprises make a fairer contribution to national budgets.[122]

Yet, decisive measures must still be formulated in order to tackle the growing problem of public indebtedness, notably in the North, which harms employment by promoting high interest rates, reducing the scope for national demand management, and freezing measures aimed at enhancing investment, productivity, and human development.

International cooperation to promote lower interest rates. High interest rates have a negative impact on investment decisions made by firms. The constraints facing governments in lowering interest rates are many.

The danger of inflation, however, is currently very low, due to restrictive monetary policies and also to structural features of product markets: increased competition means that increased demand will be met, not by increasing prices (which can only occur in a semi-monopolistic context), but by producing more goods.

A concerted effort to maintain low interest rates would promote growth and investment without putting undue pressure on any single currency. Again, cooperation depends on the extent to which each country values the fight against unemployment.

In the long run the debate over creating a new Bretton Woods or alternatives to flexible exchange rates should be reopened if, as some observers believe, there is currently "an inconsistency between free trade, free capital flows and full employment".[123] Indeed, the present system of flexible rates and free capital movements is biased towards higher interest rates (because currencies compete for international money) and against current account deficits, which result when countries attempt to expand demand.

The menu of options for a new international monetary system should thus be reopened in view of the new situation and of the apparent inability of the present arrangements to support the broader goals of full employment and sustainable human development.[124]

Promoting global citizenship in the fight against unemployment

Shifting the value debate to the global arena. If international action holds the key to any breakthrough in the fight for employment, citizens should be made aware of it and should be empowered to present and debate their policy preferences in the forums where such decisions are made. Now, however, the perceptions of ordinary citizens are still focused on national politics. Faced with a "no alternative" message from policy-makers and with the complexity of the issues involved, most people end up feeling helpless and disillusioned, and concentrate instead on more petty or sensational news— or embracing conspiracy theories or scapegoats (in Europe, immigrants, in the United States "big government"). To some degree, the worker who demonstrates against the IMF in Latin America has a more accurate perception of where real decision-making power lies than the newspaper editor who persistently runs front page stories on the meandering debates and petty rivalries of national politics.

Citizens should be made aware that decisions made in international forums will influence their future. Decisions made in other countries will also affect their employment and income prospects—a realization that has long been effective in matters of security, but not yet in economics.

Moreover, since cooperation in economic matters is crucial for defeating the competitive policies that lead to everyone becoming worse off, national policy-makers need to be rewarded when they rise above their national views and preferences and negotiate workable agreements in the common interest. Only an educated citizenry can provide such electoral incentives.

Since political representation of people, rather than states, is still embryonic at the international level, the participation of citizens through civil society organizations should be enhanced. More broadly, journalists, teachers, politicians, academics, and opinion-makers should strive to promote an understanding of global economic issues and how they affect the lives of ordinary citizens. An educated public will be better placed to understand the alternatives that exist. From that pool of informed citizens, leaders of civil society will emerge that will be able to bring to bear on economic debates the imperatives of human development and the value preferences of ordinary citizens.

From "trade unions" to "labour unions". Trade unions have been accused of delaying necessary adjustments and therefore of thwarting progress and endangering the future of the states and firms in which they have been active. Yet, comparative studies show that the more centralized and powerful labour unions are, the more they are able to consider the global picture and their place in it, to assess the costs and risks of each policy option, and, ultimately, to make responsible demands for their workers.[125]

Moreover, just as business can claim that its interests largely overlap with those of the larger community because of a "trickle down" effect, in the same way labour unions may be said to enhance the general good by promoting their own interests. In particular, they ensure that wages keep up with productivity increases, that incomes, and therefore consumer demand, do not fall behind, and that governments maintain their commitments to promoting human security. They are, among other things, instrumental in resisting the slide towards greater inequality. One of the features of the *World Bank Development Report 1995* that most struck international observers was that it contained a positive assessment of the role of trade unions and recommended enhancing this role.[126] The World Bank had previously held that trade unions create undesirable rigidities in the labour market.

Too often, however, attempts are made to pitch the interests of those currently employed against the interests of those seeking work. Lowering standards for the former, it is argued, will generate more employment for the latter. In fact, as we have seen, the competitive lowering of labour standards and social policies is a game in which all stand to lose. Therefore it is important to foster the emergence of broader-based labour unions that would represent the entire work force, whether employed or not.

These new labour unions should ensure that their voices are heard in global economic policy-making forums. They should also coordinate with their counterparts in developing economies in order to counteract the competitive pressures against workers' rights.

The emergence of the new service and information economy and the rise of self-employment may present a challenge for old style trade-unionism; but it also presents opportunities for unions to become the focal points of efforts to articulate concrete proposals in defence of human security and economic participation for all.

5.
Conclusions

This paper has argued that the current unemployment crisis compels us to look beyond the nation-state and beyond labour market theories, to the signals and incentives that lead actors in the world economy to make decisions inimical to global employment prospects. These incentives are shaped by structural changes in the spheres of finance, production and values. Therefore strategies to combat unemployment should go beyond traditional remedies, that have emphasized mere country-level adjustments in labour markets, and should address the growing discrepancy between a global market and fragmented states, and the distortions this creates.

A review of national and international policies to combat unemployment shows the interdependency between these two levels of policy-making: states need to cooperate in order to restore a measure of policy-making capability in economic matters. Likewise, the source and possible remedies for the fiscal crisis of states lie in the international sphere.

At the national level, immediate efforts should concentrate on improving the availability of credit for small scale enterprises; removing tax disincentives to employment; and reversing the growing imbalance between the overworked and the unemployed, by encouraging work sharing. Those measures could largely be formulated in such a way that they are neutral for national budgets. Other measures, such as promoting education, infrastructure and social services will be more difficult to implement, unless coordinated action is taken to mitigate the effects of fiscal deficits.

At the international level, states should actively cooperate, not only to reduce inflation, but also to enhance demand and lower interest rates, both of which have crucial effects on employment. Global dialogue should also be promoted, in order to involve ordinary citizens in global policy-making, and to present policy-makers with clear and feasible alternatives.

This global dialogue could also involve more innovative proposals, such as discussions of alternative monetary systems, or proposals to solve growing public indebtedness in the North and in the South.

SUGGESTIONS FOR FURTHER RESEARCH

In order to enhance policy efficiency and promote innovative solutions, more research needs to be done on various aspects of the global political economy of employment, and the effects of competition between states and between firms, in particular on the following:

The consistency between economic growth and human development

More research is needed on the phenomenon of jobless growth. How do growth and employment vary in relation to each other? Is there a declining growth elasticity of employment? Is this phenomenon apparent in most economies, or only in a limited sample?

A systematic exploration of the "edges" of work is also called for, as mentioned in the introduction. Can one quantify the value of unremunerated work? What are the trends, in this respect? With the rise in unemployment, are we witnessing the growth of a parallel economy, rather than its disappearance? How do disguised unemployment, unremunerated work and the informal economy relate to each other? Which one of these phenomena is most significant, from a human development viewpoint? What are the newly emerging concepts and policy proposals?

Improving global labour conditions and wages

Is the reduction in social gains in industrial countries inevitable? Or could labour conditions and wages in all countries improve, with those in developing countries improving faster than others?

The whole question of the effects of trade and technology on global employment needs further elaboration and testing. How can we specify the macroeconomic conditions needed for trade and technology to have a positive effect on employment? Is there a threshold of global demand under which technological improvements and international trade could lead to a net loss of jobs at current labour prices?

How can one test the hypothesis that the uncoordinated search for competitiveness may, in certain circumstances, hinder employment?

Policy-making and the global economy
More empirical work is needed on the effects that the internationalization of firms has on the financial situation of states. Can one document a gap globally between growing private returns and stagnating tax revenues? Could the tax-saving benefits of globalization for firms help explain why foreign direct investment and international trade (much of it intrafirm) have grown much faster than world GNP? Data is missing in this important area, which is at the heart of the dilemma of divided states in a global market.

On the policy side, what is the scope for global policy coordination to help restore national sovereignty in addressing employment issues? If there were such coordination, what would be the most appropriate forum, and how could one ensure proper representation of all countries?

As far as national policy-making is concerned, research should focus on policy trade-offs, creatively seeking solutions to minimize these trade-offs and enhance human development and opportunities.

Recent experiments in national employment policies should be reviewed and assessed, for example pro-labour shifts in national tax systems, or other pro-labour incentive policies.

The status and role of trade unions could also be reviewed: what are examples of transitions from "trade unions" to "labour-unions" as defined earlier? What are the lessons gained?

The pursuit of employment and sustainable human development in the face of an increasingly dysfunctional world economy thus requires a comprehensive diagnosis, the formulation of innovative and feasible solutions, and the pursuit of an ongoing policy dialogue.

Notes

1. This study owes its title, and more, to the book by John Stopford and Susan Strange, *Rival States, Rival Firms: Competition for World Market Shares*. (Cambridge: Cambridge University Press. 1993.) In addition, many thanks are due for comments and suggestions, or for assistance in collecting material and statistics, to Yilmaz Akyuz, Meghnad Desai, John Eatwell, Leo Goldstone, Keith Griffin, Shareen Hertel, Inge Kaul, Aziz Rachman Khan, John Lawrence, Laura MacQuade, Sanjay Reddy, Sophie Tremolet and the participants of a UNDP Development Committee seminar. Neither the reviewers nor UNDP bear final responsibility for this study.

2. For example, Susan Strange, *States and Markets*. London: Pinter. 1988.

3. For a study of disguised unemployment, see John Eatwell, "Disguised Unemployment: The G-7 Experience." UNCTAD Discussion Papers No. 106. Geneva: United Nations Conference on Trade and Development, November 1995.

4. United Nations, *World Economic and Social Survey 1995—Current Trends and Policies in the World Economy*. New York: Department for Economic and Social Information and Policy Analysis, United Nations, 1995. pp. 2 and 35.

5. United Nations 1995, p. 235. See note 4.

6. United Nations Development Programme, *Human Development Report 1993*. New York and Oxford: Oxford University Press. 1993. pp. 3, 34–37.

7. European Union's 1995 Annual Employment Report, as quoted in "EU Faces Stagnant Job Market For Next Two Years." *Financial Times*, 26 July 1995.

8. United Nations 1995, p. 300. See note 4.

9. International Labour Organization, *World Employment 1995, An ILO Report*.

Geneva: International Labour Organization. 1995. pp. 65 and 66.

10. International Labour Organization 1995, p. 66. See note 9.

11. United Nations 1995, p. 18. See note 4.

12. United Nations 1995, p. 62, 65. See note 4.

13. United Nations 1995, p. 61. See note 4.

14. International Labour Organization, "Promoting Employment: Report of the Director-General." International Labour Conference, 82nd Session 1995. Geneva: ILO. 1995, p. 93.

15. See for example A. Patrick L. Minford, "Has Labour Market Economics Achieved a Synthesis?" *The Economic Journal* 103: 1050–1056. 1993.

16. "Wage Dispersion and Growth in the United States." *Finance and Development,* June 1995. p. 16. "The Wealth Gap is Real and It's Growing." *New York Times,* 22 August 1995.

17. "Inequality: For Richer, For Poorer." *The Economist,* 5 November 1994. p. 19.

18. "Wage Dispersion and Growth in the United States." *Finance and Development,* June 1995. p. 16..

19. Ibid., p. 20.

20. International Labour Organization 1995, p. 88. See note 9.

21. The World Bank, *Workers in an Integrating World (World Development Report 1995),* Oxford and Washington, D.C.: Oxford University Press. 1995. p. 120.

22. "Twice the Workers, Twice the Productivity." *World Bank Research Bulletin,* August–October. 1995. p. 6.

23. See also Paul Krugman, "Europe Jobless, America Penniless?" *Foreign Policy* 95: 19–34. 1994.

24. Thomas J. Carter, "Efficiency Wages: Employment Versus Welfare." *Southern Economic Journal,* July 1995. See also note 4, p. 229.

25. United Nations 1995, p. 229.

26. Edward N. Wolff, *Top Heavy: A Study of the Increasing Inequality of Wealth in America.* New York: The Twentieth Century Fund Press. 1995.

27. "Wage Dispersion and Growth in the United States." *Finance and Development,* June 1995. p. 18.

28. Ray Marshall, "The Global Jobs Crisis." *Foreign Policy* Fall: 54. 1995.

29. "It Was a Banner Year for Profit." *Fortune,* 7 August 1995. p. 130.

30. See Organisation for Economic Co-operation and Development (OECD), *Employment Outlook.* Paris: OECD. 1995. pp. 8–15.

31. "The Wage Squeeze." *Business Week,* 17 July 1995. pp. 54–62.

32. It may also be that "jobless growth" in the United States is due to the presence of significant "disguised unemployment". As the demand for labour increases in a recovery, people move from low-productivity, subsistence jobs (which are nevertheless considered "jobs" for statistical purposes) to high-productivity jobs. In pure quantitative terms, however, this effect is invisible. See John Eatwell, "Disguised Unemployment: The G-7 Experience." UNCTAD Discussion Papers No. 106. Geneva: United Nations Conference on Trade and Development, November 1995.

33. International Labour Organization 1995, pp. 84–87. See note 9.

34. World Bank 1995. See note 21.

35. See for example Nancy Birdsall, David Ross and Richard Sabot, "Inequality and Growth Reconsidered: Lessons from East Asia." *The World Bank Economic Review* 9 (3): 477–508.

36. "Disguised unemployment" is more and more a reality in the North, too. Between 1979 and 1987, some 80% of the jobs created in the United Kingdom, and 50% of the jobs created in the United States, were low-productivity and low-pay. See note 3, pp. vii and 209–212.

37. International Labour Organization 1995, p. 87. See note 9.

38. International Labour Organization 1995, pp. 93–97. See note 9.

39. "Jobs: How a Simple but Effective Service Fulfills Employment and Social Needs: Working to Spice the Bombay Mix." *Financial Times*, 23 June 1995.

40. Human Development Report of the Republic of Moldova, p. 33. 1995.

41. Ray Barrell, Julian Morgan and Nigel Pain, "The Employment Effects of the Maastricht Fiscal Criteria." National Institute of Economic and Social Research, Discussion Paper No. 81, June 1995.

42. International Labour Organization 1995, p. 130. See note 9.

43. "Japan's Jobless Rate at Highest Level Ever." *New York Times*, 31 May 1995; "Japanese Jobless Rate Rises to a Record 3.4%." *Financial Times*, 27 December 1995.

44. "Yen's Rise Catastrophic, Say Japanese Business Leaders." *Financial Times*, 20 April 1995.

45. International Labour Organization 1995, p. 106. See note 9.

46. On the issue of unemployment in Eastern Europe see for example Rudiger Dornbusch, Wilhelm Nolling and Richard Layard, eds., *Postwar Economic Reconstruction and Lessons for the East Today*. Cambridge, Mass.: Cambridge University Press. 1993. Also see Olivier Blanchard, Maxim Boycko, Marek Dabrowski, Richard Layard and Andrei Shleifer, *Post-Communist Reform: Pain and Progress*. Cambridge, Mass.: MIT Press 1993.

47. "Argentine Jobless Level At New High." *Financial Times*, 21 July 1995.

48. See for example Paul Streeten. ed., *Beyond Adjustment: The Asian Experience.* Washington, D.C.: International Monetary Fund. 1988. See also United Nations Development Programme, *Stabilization and Adjustment.* New York. 1991.

49. International Labour Organization 1995, p. 66. See note 9.

50. United Nations 1995, p. 235. See note 4.

51. United Nations, *World's Women's Statistics 1995.* New York. 1995. p. 110.

52. Ibid., p. 112.

53. "Unemployment at Record 3.4% in November." *Financial Times*, 27 December 1995.

54. Patrick Minford, quoted in "Wage Pressures from South." *Financial Times*, 1 June 1995.

55. "Haunted by the Trade Specter." *Financial Times*, 24 July 1995. A forthcoming publication of the Institute of International Economics by William Cline provides a more thorough synthesis of this literature.

56. *Promoting Employment, Report of the Director-General, International Labour Conference.* Geneva: International Labour Organization. 1995. p. 27.

57. "It Was a Banner Year for Profit." *Fortune*, 7 August 1995. p. 134.

58. See also "Companies' Profits Grew 15%, With Boost From Exports." *Wall Street Journal*, 7 August 1995. p. A1.

59. See Jagdish Bhagwati, "'Paupers' Trade View Has Not Been Proven." *Financial Times*, 4 August 1995, letter to the Editor. See also Paul Krugman and Robert Lawrence, "Trade, Jobs and Wages." NBER Working Paper No. 4478. Cambridge, Mass.: National Bureau of Economic Research, Washington, D.C.: World Bank. 1995. p. 56.

60. See Centre for Economic Policy Research (CEPR), *Unemployment: Choices for Europe.* London: CEPR. 1995. p. 50.

61. This is the classical argument in favour of the "benign" nature of technological advances. For a clear summary, see for example "One Lump of Two?" *The Economist*, 25 November 1995. p. 67–68.

62. The 1995 UNCTAD Trade and Development Report (see note 73) also attempts to look beyond trade and technology: "the real question, in both cases [technology and international trade] is why it has been so difficult for the labour displaced to be redeployed at remunerative wages elsewhere in the economy—as in the Golden Age of the 1950's and 1960's."

63. Susan Strange, *States and Markets.* London: Pinter. 1988.

64. International Labour Organization 1995, pp. 193–200. See note 9.

65. The Universal Declaration of Human Rights adopted in 1948 for example stipulates in article 23 that "everyone has the right to work, to free choice of employment, to just and favourable conditions of work and to protection against unemployment".

66. Brazilian textile producers, for example, are now complaining about cheap imports from China and Republica of Korea. See "Textile Industry Cries Afoul: Cheap Imports Alarm Brazil Business." *Financial Times*, 26 September 1995.

67. Data by the Economic Policy Institute.

68. "Leaky Boats on the Rising Tide." *New York Times*, 29 August 1995; see also note 73, p. 64.

69. Klaus Schwab and C. Smadja, "The New Rules of the Game in a World of Many Players." *Harvard Business Review*, November 1994.

70. Calculations done by World Statistics, New York, from World Bank and OECD data.

71. "Costly." *The Economist*, 8 October 1994. p.59.

72. Truman F. Bewley, "A Depressed Labour Market As Explained By Participants." *American Economic Review*, May 1995. pp. 250–254.

73. "Companies' Profits Grew 15%, With Boost From Exports." *Wall Street Journal*, 7 August 1995.

74. John Stopford and Susan Strange, *Rival States, Rival Firms: Competition for World Market Shares*. Cambridge: Cambridge University Press. 1993. More and more the institutions concerned with foreign affairs (including secret services) are being used to promote economic, rather than political or military objectives.

75. United Nations Conference on Trade and Development, *Trade and Development Report, 1995*. Geneva: UNCTAD. 1995. p. vi.

76. Bank for International Settlements, Sixty–Fourth Annual Report, 1994. p. 28.

77. UNCTAD. 1995, p. 159. See note 73.

78. See Edmund S. Phelps and Jean-Pierre Fitoussi, *The Slump in Europe*. New York: Basil Blackwell. 1988. See also Edmund S. Phelps, *Structural Slumps: The Modern Equilibrium Theory of Unemployment, Interest and Assets*. Cambridge, Mass.: Harvard University Press. 1994.

79. See UNCTAD 1995 (note 73) and Sharon J. Erenburg, "The Relationship Between Public and Private Investment." Working Paper No.85, Washington University in Saint Louis. 1993. pp. 15–16.

80. UNCTAD 1995, p. 179. See note 73.

81. Indeed, demand expectations (which influence the expected returns on

investment) are sometimes even more powerful than interest rates in determining whether or not a firm will undertake production (and hence hire labour). The Depression of the 1930s, for example, lasted because of low demand expectations, and in spite of low interest rates.

82. Some of these difficulties are detectable for example in World Bank 1995 (see note 21).

83. EU White Paper, pp. 140–141.

84. International Labour Organization 1995, pp. 144–158 (see note 9); United Nations 1995, pp. 242–247 (see note 4).

85. Paul Krugman, "Europe Jobless, America Penniless?" *Foreign Policy* 95: 24. 1994.

86. UNCTAD 1995, pp. 164–169. See note 21.

87. UNCTAD 1995, p. vii. See note 21.

88. Olivier Blanchard and Juan F. Jimeno, "Structural Unemployment: Spain versus Portugal." *American Economic Review*, May 1995. pp. 212–218.

89. See for example "Minimum Wage, Maximum Fuss." *The Economist*, 8 April 1995. p. 69. See also "Why Not Rent Control?" *The Economist*, 8 April 1995. p. 70. Recently a group of 101 economists, including several Nobel prize winners, formally called for a substantive raise in the United States minimum wage, citing several studies showing that the raise would barely affect employment and prices. See "Economists Back Proposal To Lift Minimum Wage." *Wall Street Journal*, 3 October 1995.

90. Robert Reich, "Why Economic Growth Is Not Enough." *Financial Times*, 5 June 1995.

91. United Nations 1995, p. 246. See note 4. In the case of the United Kingdom, however, it seems that more and better training can improve employment prospects ("Skills in Short Supply, Say Bosses." *Financial Times*, 21 December 1995. p. 7.)

92. See Jens Bastian: "Work Sharing: the Reappearance of a Timely Idea" in The Political Quarterly, 1994, pp. 302–312; "Job-Sharing: Box and Cox", The Economist, 6 August 1994, p. 56.

93. "Time Flies, But Where Does It Go?" *New York Times*, 6 September 1995.

94. "Work Culture That Brings No Satisfaction." *Financial Times*, 25 August 1995.

95. "An Unhealthy Working Week." *Financial Times*, 27 December 1995.

96. "When do Workers Have Time for Family Life?" *Financial Times*, 29–30 July 1995. p. iii.

97. "Sharing the Burden." *The Economist*, 13 November 1993. p. 18.

98. "Russian Shares Can Guarantee Adventure." *Financial Times*, 19 September 1995.

99. Geoffrey Carliner, *Reducing Global Unemployment*. Washington, D.C.: Overseas Development Council. 1995. p.14.

100. See the current ODS initiative on "A New Relationship Between Private Sector Finance and Development."

101. "Tax Surcharge to Fund French Jobs and Welfare." *Financial Times*, 22 June 1995; "Dutch Seek Jobs From Tax Cuts in Budget." *Financial Times*, 20 September 1995; "Labour Plans Utility Levy." *Financial Times*, 26 September 1995.

102. Organisation for Economic Cooperation and Development (OECD), *OECD Economic Outlook*. Paris: OECD. 1995. p. 72.

103. Samuel Bentolina and Olivier Blanchard, "Spanish Unemployment." *Economic Policy* 10. 1990.

104. See for example Olivier Blanchard and Lawrence Summers, "Hysteresis and the European Unemployment Problem." In Stanley Fischer, ed., *Macroeconomics Annual, 1986*. Cambridge, Mass.: MIT Press. 1986. pp. 15–78.

105. "IMF Policies 'Negative' For East." *Financial Times*, 22 August 1995.

106. See Dharam Ghai and Cynthia Hewitt de Alcantara, "The Crisis of the 1980's in Sub-Saharan Africa, Latin America and the Caribbean: Economic Impact, Social Change and Political Implications." *Development and Change*, 21: 389–426. 1990. See also ODS initiative on "Socially Responsible Structural Adjustment".

107. World Bank 1995, pp. 54–56. See note 21.

108. See Ricardo Ffrench–Davis and Manuel Agosin, "Managing Capital Flows in Latin America." UNDP Conference on New and Innovative Sources of Development Cooperation, New York, 10 October 1995. See also "IMF Shifts Stance on Capital Control." *Financial Times*, 22 August 1995; International Monetary Fund, *Capital Account Convertibility*. Washington, D.C.: IMF. 1995. p. 23.

109. Examples of such negotiations are given in John Stopford and Susan Strange, *Rival States, Rival Firms*. Cambridge: Cambridge University Press. 1993.

110. International Labour Organization 1995, pp. 80–97. See note 9.

111. Public goods (such as clean air, or freedom from war) are not a good investment for private entrepreneurs, because it is impossible to charge all of those who benefit by them—short of levying a tax, which only public authorities can do.

112. John Langmore and John Quiggin, *Work For All: Full Employment in the Nineties*. Melbourne: Melbourne University Press. 1994.

113. UNCTAD 1995, p. vii. See note 73.

114. International Labour Organization 1995, pp. 96–97. See note 9.

115. Some of these proposals have been advocated by Jeremy Rifkin in *The End of Work: The Decline of the Global Labor Force and the Dawn of the Post-Market Era.* New York: G.P. Putnam's Sons. 1995.

116. Unpublished report on fiscal integration, Ministry of Finance, Directorate-General of Taxes, Paris, 12 October 1995 (quoted in *Le Canard Enchaîné*, 15 November 1995).

117. See for example Gilles Oudiz and Jeffrey Sachs, "Macroeconomic Policy Coordination Among the Industrialized Economies." Brookings Paper on Economic Activity, No. 1. Washington, D.C.: Brookings University. 1984. See also Jeffrey Sachs and Warwick J. McKibbin, "Macroeconomic Policies in the OECD and LDC External Adjustment." NBER Working Paper No. 1255. Cambridge, Mass.: National Bureau of Economic Research. 1985.

118. Ray Marshall, "The Global Job Crisis." *Foreign Policy*, Fall 1995, p. 54.

119. See Robert Putnam and Nicholas Bayne, *Hanging Together: Cooperation and Conflict in the Seven Power Summits.* Cambridge, Mass.: Harvard University Press. 1987.

120. "Central Banks Celebrate Victory Over Markets." *Financial Times*, 19–20 August 1995.

121. This conclusion emerged from the conference "Labor Rights In A Global Economy", Friedrich Ebert Stiftung/Bread for the World, New York, 4 December 1995.

122. "US Tax Move Alarms Multinational Groups." *Financial Times*, 15 August 1995. See also Gary Clyde Hufbauer, with Joanna M. van Rooij, *U.S. Taxation of International Income: Blueprint for Reform.* Washington, D.C.: Institute for International Economics. 1992.

123. International Labour Organization, "Promoting Employment: Report of the Director-General." International Labour Conference, 1995.

124. UNCTAD 1995, p. 131. See note 73. For a recent example of such debates, see for example Peter Kenen, ed., *Managing the World Economy, Fifty Years After Bretton Woods.* Washington, D.C.: Institute for International Economics. 1994. See also the Report of the Bretton Woods Committee, *Bretton Woods: Looking to the Future.* Washington, D.C. 1994.

125. Charles R. Bean, "European Unemployment: a Survey." *Journal of Economic Literature.* 23. 1994.

126. World Bank 1995, pp. 79–86. See note 21.

Author's Biographical Note

Isabelle Grunberg is a Senior Policy Analyst at the Office of Development Studies. Formerly, she was Associate Director of the Secretariat of the Independent Working Group on the Future of the United Nations and a MacArthur Fellow and Lecturer at Yale University. She has also been a lecturer at the London School of Economics and the Institut d'Etudes Politiques in Paris—two institutions from which she earned postgraduate degrees in economics and international relations. She has also received a French doctoral equivalent (agrégation) from the Sorbonne University and the Ecole Normale Supérieure.